"In this book, Lynn really speaks to teachers, recognising the lack of initial training to support the positive teaching of autistic children, but also the crucial part teachers and para-professionals can play in supporting autistic children to thrive. What makes this book a 'must read' is its focus on autistic voices, which brings examples to life and the fact that the practical strategies offered for primary schools can be immediately put into practice."

– **Nicola Crossley**, CEO NAS Academies Trust and National SEND representative for ASCL

"Lynn recognises that knowing how best to meet autistic students' needs may often feel daunting, particularly in busy, demanding classrooms. As a specialist teacher, Lynn's desire to bring out the best in every pupil, matches that of her readers. Here she shares her wealth of knowledge and experience of supporting autistic students, providing highly practical, tried-and-tested, 'lived-experience' advice and examples, relevant for teachers, school support staff, as well as consulting professionals, including Educational Psychologists, SLTs and OTs. This resource also offers an easily accessible update on current thinking around autistic experiences, developing a wider understanding of Neurodiversity within education, and further helping to reduce the Double Empathy gap."

– **Lisa Chapman**, Lead Speech and Language Therapist at BeeU: Child & Adolescent Mental Health Services, Midlands Partnership NHS Foundation Trust

"This is a book that should be in every staff room. Its clarity and plethora of practical easy to implement strategies will enhance teachers' inclusive practice. It is also a bible for understanding Autism in current times."

– **Sally Glossop**, Lead for the Graduated Response Herts county council

"Lynn's dedication to making the world a better place for autistic people shines through this book from every page. This, combined with her understanding of what it is like to be a teacher in a busy classroom with a million things on your to-do list already, makes this book a super practical guide. If you want to do better by the autistic children in your classroom then this is the book for you."

– **Joanna Grace**, Sensory Engagement and Inclusion specialist and Founder of The Sensory Projects

"Lynn's research and work with autistic people has once again informed her excellent books. The work with autistic young people, doing 'what's right for me' is outstanding in achieving best practice for those young people and beyond to their families and classmates. I would recommend both the primary and secondary editions to inform and enable all school staff to fully understand and support the young people in their care."

– **Dawn Brown**, SEND Assistant Head, Hertfordshire

"School staff generally receive such little training about autism that becoming an expert in teaching autistic pupils may seem out of reach. This brilliant book provides a solution, with clear explanations of autistic differences and potential barriers to learning, plus multiple strategies to support autistic children in school. What makes it so special, however, are the quotes and diversity of experiences that Lynn shares. These evidence autistic pupils as unique and neurodivergent, not disordered and encourage practitioners to see the power of their curiosity and care as the route to helping these children thrive."

– **Ruth Moyse**, Director and Associate Consultant, AT-Autism

"What do we do when faced with a class of children who don't learn how we teach? A question posed as you start reading that resonates. With an increasing number of our children being diagnosed with Autism, teachers are seeking more support on how to help. Reading this book will develop your understanding around the real challenges autistic children may be faced with daily. As you read, you will become more aware of how topics such as bullying, sensory differences, communication and engaging with the curriculum can affect even our youngest children. A section on 'masking' is useful when discussing concerns raised by parents. The voice of autistic children has been captured and it is their perspective alongside the deeper understanding gained that encourages reflections on current practice and an eagerness to think differently about how some lessons and the school day may be presented to our children."

– **Julie Osbaldeston**, Deputy Headteacher and SENDCo, Freshfield Primary School

"As an autistic children's occupational therapist, specialising in neurodivergent affirming practice I spend a great deal of time supporting autistic children, their parents and teachers. I have followed Lynn's work via social media interactions for a number of years and know how valued her input is to the autistic and educational communities. This book feels so appropriate for the time, where Primary SENCOs, Inclusion Leads and pastoral staff need to know quickly and effectively how to support neurodivergent children to build healthy foundations for not only their educational outcomes but mental health and wellbeing."

– **Holly Sprake-Hill**, Neurodivergence Specialist, Sparkle Occupational Therapy

All About Autism (Primary) is accompanied by a number of printable online materials, designed to ensure this resource best supports your professional needs.

Go to https://resourcecentre.routledge.com/speechmark and click on the cover of this book.

Answer the question prompt using your copy of the book to gain access to the online content.

ALL ABOUT AUTISM

All About Autism is an accessible and informative guide for primary school teachers, designed to increase their knowledge and understanding of autism and enhance their toolkit with practical, adaptable strategies to support autistic children in their care.

The book initially explores key traits and terminology, debunks myths and misconceptions, and shines a light on the strengths and abilities of autistic learners. It then introduces readers to a range of easy-to-implement ideas for practice and concrete solutions to provide further support, all with the child at the heart. *All About Autism* includes:

- Practical strategies tailored to the primary key stages with current research broken down into easily digestible chunks.
- Guidance on a range of topics, from the importance of play for developing communication and supporting sensory needs to building peer relationships and social awareness for all.
- Strategies to create an autistic-friendly environment and teach in a way that caters to students with different ways of learning.
- Advice for helping autistic learners with problem solving and managing demands, tests and bridging the gap between primary and secondary school.
- Easy to dip in and out of chapters with signposting to further research, resources and support.

Taking a celebratory approach, the guide focuses on difference rather than deficit and weaves together the voices of autistic children and parents alongside practical examples of what high-quality and adapted teaching should look like. It will be essential reading for all primary school educators, SENCOs and parents who are supporting autistic learners, aged 4-11.

Lynn McCann has been a teacher for 32 years and in that time has worked as a mainstream teacher, SENCO and for eight years was a class and outreach teacher in an autism specialist school. She set up Reachout ASC in 2014 after realising that there was a great need for good, practical, specialist support in mainstream schools. It is an independent service that specialises in autism, ADHD and PDA support, with children's voices at the heart of all they do.

ALL ABOUT SEND

Series Advisor: Natalie Packer

All About SEND provides busy teachers and SENCOs with essential guidance and practical strategies to effectively support learner with special educational needs and disabilities. Each accessible and informative book focuses on a common area of need and explores key traits and terminology, debunks myths and misconceptions, and introduces readers to a range of easy-to-implement ideas for practice and concrete solutions to everyday challenges.

ALL ABOUT AUTISM
A Practical Guide for Primary Teachers
Lynn McCann

ALL ABOUT AUTISM
A Practical Guide for Secondary Teachers
Lynn McCann

ALL ABOUT AUTISM

A PRACTICAL GUIDE FOR PRIMARY TEACHERS

Lynn McCann

LONDON AND NEW YORK

Designed cover image: © Getty Images

First published 2023
by Routledge
4 Park Square, Milton Park, Abingdon, Oxon OX14 4RN

and by Routledge
605 Third Avenue, New York, NY 10158

Routledge is an imprint of the Taylor & Francis Group, an informa business

© 2023 Lynn McCann

British Library Cataloguing-in-Publication Data
A catalogue record for this book is available from the British Library

ISBN: 978-1-032-24778-6 (hbk)
ISBN: 978-1-032-24779-3 (pbk)
ISBN: 978-1-003-28006-4 (ebk)

DOI: 10.4324/9781003280064

Typeset in Interstate
by Deanta Global Publishing Services, Chennai, India

Access the online resources: https://resourcecentre.routledge.com/ speechmark

CONTENTS

FOREWORD

All teachers are teachers of learners with Special Educational Needs and Disabilities (SEND). Those professionals who work in truly inclusive schools will understand that SEND is everyone's responsibility. However, the situation has not always been like this. When I started my teaching career

32 years ago, learners who had additional needs were more likely to be seen as the responsibility of the Special Educational Needs Coordinator (SENCO). As the person in school who 'held' the SEND knowledge and expertise, the SENCO would often be a lone force in championing, and meeting, the needs of this particular group of learners.

The picture in education is somewhat different today. The profile of the children and young people we teach continues to change. The impact of the Covid pandemic, for example, has led to an increase in those identified with gaps in their learning, or with mental health concerns. The number of learners with complex needs being educated within mainstream schools also continues to rise. As professionals, we now have a greater awareness and understanding of some of the challenges our learners face and, as a result, are more determined to do our best to support them to achieve. We understand that this cannot be the role of one person – the SENCO – alone. Every teacher needs to be a teacher of SEND.

Teaching learners with SEND may be one of the most rewarding things you ever do in your classroom. When you observe a learner who has really struggled to grasp a new idea or concept finally achieve their 'lightbulb moment,' it's all the more sweet knowing the amount of effort they have put in to get there. However, teaching learners with SEND can also be one of the most challenging aspects of your career. In a 2019 survey[1] carried out by the Department for Education (DfE) in England, the level of confidence amongst teachers in supporting learners with SEND was reported as very low. Relevant professional development in this area is, at best, patchy; only 41% of the teachers surveyed by the DfE felt there was sufficient SEND training in place for all teachers.

So how do we overcome this challenge? Evidence suggests that the best place to start is through the delivery of inclusive, High Quality Teaching (HQT). As the Education Endowment Foundation (EEF) report[2] tells us, there is no 'magic bullet' for teaching learners with SEND and to a great extent, good teaching for those with SEND is good teaching for all. This means we need to develop a repertoire of effective teaching strategies such as scaffolding, explicit instruction and use of technology, then use these strategies flexibly to meet the needs of individuals or groups of learners.

Although a focus on effective, HQT in the classroom is the starting point, some learners will require more specific teaching methods to meet their individual needs. There is no substitute for really getting to know a child or young person so you can fully understand their personal strengths, potential barriers to learning and what works for them in the classroom. However, it can still be helpful for us as professionals to develop a more general understanding of some of the common areas of need we are likely to come across and to have a range of strategies we can try implementing within our practice. This is where *All About SEND* can help.

The *All About SEND* series of books aims to support every teacher to be a teacher of SEND. Each book has been designed to enable teachers, and other professionals such as support staff, to develop their knowledge and understanding of how to effectively promote teaching and learning for those with identified areas of need. The books provide essential information and a range of practical strategies for supporting learners in the classroom. Written by expert practitioners, the guidance has been informed by a wealth of first-hand experience, with the views of children and young people with SEND and their parents taking centre stage.

In this book, *All About Autism*, the author Lynn McCann provides essential guidance on supporting autistic learners in the primary classroom. As Director of Reachout ASC autism outreach service, Lynn has vast experience of working directly with autistic learners and their families and in supporting schools to develop excellent autism-friendly practice. Written from a very child-centred viewpoint, *All About Autism* provides a range of extremely practical, tried-and-tested ideas based on what really works for autistic learners in the classroom.

Thank you for choosing to read this book and for embracing the challenge of responsibility: every teacher a teacher of SEND.

Natalie Packer

All About SEND Series Advisor
SEND Consultant, Director of NPEC Ltd.
@NataliePacker

NOTES

1 https://assets.publishing.service.gov.uk/government/uploads/system/uploads/attachment_data/file/1063620/SEND_review_right_support_right_place_right_time_accessible.pdf pg. 42.
2 https://educationendowmentfoundation.org.uk/education-evidence/guidance-reports/send.

ACKNOWLEDGEMENTS

Writing any book like this cannot happen without the help of the teachers, parents and most of all the autistic children I have worked with over the past ten years or more. Working with so many dedicated people who are committed to making school successful for all children has been a joy. We all know the realities of an education system still trying to recover from a pandemic as I write this in 2022, and a SEND system that seems increasingly unable to provide the resources to make education accessible and successful for all children. But we teachers have a lot of creativity and hope. We do this job because we want to see children thrive and I hope this book will help you understand and make that difference for your autistic pupils this year and every year. Thank you for reading this book and wanting to learn from the children and teachers I have worked with in their schools.

I want to thank the following schools who have given me permission to use scenarios from their practice in this book:

Freshfield Primary School, Formby, Merseyside
St Leonard's CE Primary School, Padiham, Lancashire
Ellel St John's CE Primary School, Galgate, Lancashire
Christ Church CE Primary School, Lancaster, Lancashire

And the following organisations or individuals who have given me permission to use quotes from their surveys and children who are autistic:

Spectrum Gaming (Andy Smith and his team) www.spectrum-gaming.net
Faith Mummy Facebook page (Miriam Gwynne and her daughter Naomi)
www.facebook.com/Faithmummy1

And the pupils I have worked with over the past ten years: many of them wanted to remain anonymous but a few wanted their names included:

Hope, aged 10
Jemima, aged 11

Autistic adults I have supported or worked with:

Cristina Mylroie
Jackson Watkinson
Hilary Forbes
Dean Beadle

And those who wished to remain anonymous.
    I thank you all with all my heart. I could never have written this without you. I hope I have been faithful to your words and your school experiences, and that this book will help teachers for many years to come.
    Thanks to Stephen, Sio and Matt, my wonderful family.
    And to my English teacher, Mr Terry Morgan from 1981–1984, who believed I could be a writer.

INTRODUCTION

Teachers are at the heart of any child's educational experience and the relationships we have with our pupils can impact them for the rest of their lives. Can you think back to something a teacher once said to you? Whether it was something negative, such as "You'll never make a runner" (once said to my husband who spent 20 years of his life doing fell running races and marathons), or something positive, such as "You would make a great teacher" (said to me by my English teacher when I was a painfully quiet and anxious 14-year-old).

In our daily classroom practice, we don't often get much time to reflect or to think differently about the way we teach or the individual needs and strengths of our pupils. And when we are forced to have to, it is often because there are behaviour or mental health issues that have caused a crisis. Most of the teachers I've ever met or worked with went into teaching to make a positive difference to children's lives and, despite the pressures and stress of the enormous daily demands, still want to invest in all pupils' lives.

So, what do we do when faced with a class that includes children who learn in ways that are different from how teachers typically teach? They may have a diagnosis or, more often, they are yet to be diagnosed and we are trying to respond to parental concerns and the challenges of having to show progress in learning for a child who may be struggling. There may be disruptions to our hours of carefully planned lessons which have an effect other children's learning. Or it could be the data has flagged up a child who isn't engaging, who seems withdrawn. We also work with a lot of children who work really hard to mask

DOI: 10.4324/9781003280064-1

their difficulties in school, and the school thinks they are fine ... but their parents tell a different story.

The reality is that the way we teach and are taught to teach is often not the best way for autistic children to learn. Some of that is systematic, the way we organise our schools and the expectations put on schools for certain types of results. This is often not conducive to inclusive education. The lack of training and dialogue about what inclusive education is in teacher training leaves many teachers ill equipped for the range of children they will be teaching in any class. Inclusive education often brings to mind a classroom where children of all abilities and disabilities can be taught together and benefit from the social and cultural environment of understanding and learning together.

> The importance of inclusive education is defined in its positive outcomes for all children – both with and without disabilities or other disadvantages. For example, The European Agency for Special Needs and Inclusive Education (EASNIE) (2018), has provided ample evidence that inclusive education increases social and academic opportunities for both children with and without disabilities, as well as significantly increases the likelihood that children with disabilities enrol in higher education and have better employment and life outcomes (see also Florian, Black-Hawkins and Rouse, 2017; Hehir, et al., 2016).
>
> *(Schuelka, 2018, p. 3)*

This does demand that teachers are given the flexibility to adapt and reflect on the wide variety of needs and abilities of their pupils, year by year, and be supported and trusted to make their teaching fit the needs of their pupils. If we have school leaders and government agencies that understand this, then the whole approach to inclusion can be one where all children thrive. However, without focusing on all the barriers to this, which will depend on the country you are currently teaching in, there are approaches that all teachers can use to make school a positive and successful journey for autistic students, and other children with different Special Educational Needs and Disabilities (SEND), which is what this book is about.

I started out as a mainstream primary teacher in 1991 and majored in SEND education. After 14 years of teaching in primary schools, I moved to a specialist school for autistic children with a variety of learning difficulties and whilst there I set up the school's outreach service. In 2014 I left to set up my own advisory service to mainstream schools, after seeing the huge need for support that they had. Now, nine years later, I have a team of seven people; five of us are specialist teachers, and the other three work behind the scenes to enable us to deliver the highest quality support for each autistic child we work with. We come alongside and equip their teachers and involve parents as part of the team that will help the child thrive in school. Some of our team are autistic, some are parents of autistic children and some have other neurodiverse experiences.

Throughout this book, I will be giving you examples and quotes from children who have gone through the education system and have had support that enabled them to survive, and sometimes thrive. Autistic children are often very honest and direct, and given the space to communicate and someone with the time to listen, they can give us important insights into what school is like for them and what can be done to make it better. Some autistic children struggle to find the words to communicate, and some may be non-verbal. In these cases, we (my team of autism specialist teachers and I, and the children's teachers and parents) have spent time observing and listening to the other ways that the child communicates and have brought you our best interpretation of what they seem to be communicating. Our years of listening to the insights of autistic adults, including those who do not use speech to communicate, have helped enormously with this. Although minimally verbal autistic children may still use words for self-stimulation and to try to ask you for things, the expectation to use speech for communication in school can put them at a huge disadvantage. I have worked with autistic children who are situationally mute, and we have communicated quite adequately through writing or drawing or symbols. However, many autistic children who do not speak are assumed to have learning disabilities. They are regularly sent to specialist schools, and even there they are not always offered adequate communication tools. Naoki Higashida, who wrote *The Reason I Jump*, was able to communicate after being given lessons on writing, and Jonathan Bryan, who wrote *Eye Can Write*, has a national campaign (Teach Us Too) to teach spelling and writing to non-verbal children. We don't know what intelligence children have until we can connect with how they can communicate it. It is a common mistake to underestimate autistic children because their communication system is different to ours.

> *Please don't judge us from the outside only. I don't know why we can't talk properly. But it's not that we won't talk – it's that we can't talk and we're suffering because of it.*
> (Naoki Higashida, 2014)

I want to thank all the autistic children and adults who have contributed to this book. I believe passionately that we can change the school experience for so many other children by learning from their insights. I will be brutal and tell you that so many autistic students have been utterly failed by their educational experience, and many more have barely been able to survive. Many have ended up with mental ill health and trauma, and the damage has had a limiting effect on their lives into their adult years. But occasionally there is a spark of hope. And that hope comes from teachers and teaching assistants like you who are reading this book. A teacher or teaching assistant, or even better, a head teacher and a whole school that 'gets' autism and works hard to make sure that autistic and other SEND children are given the best chance to thrive, no matter what it takes. I have worked with schools that have changed small things that make a huge difference, and sometimes big things like school routines, systems and practices – for just one child. They have seen the benefit tenfold as other children they didn't realise needed that support started to thrive too. And that is what this book will help you do. Whether as a teacher or teaching assistant working largely on your own

(I really hope you don't find yourself in this position, but it happens) or as part of a whole-school approach, what you do for your autistic pupils will never be forgotten by them. And I thank you for taking the time to investigate, understand and implement what they need. You are doing the right thing.

And if you are a parent reading this book, I hope you feel supported and understood by your child's school staff too. I hope you can all work together to do the best that is possible for your child, listen well to each other and work through the challenges together. I know children are so much better off when the relationships around them are strong and together.

WHAT WE KNOW ABOUT AUTISM

Donna Williams, an autistic woman, wrote:

> right from the start, from the time someone came up with the word 'autism,' the condition has been judged from the outside, by its appearances, and not from the inside according to how it is experienced.
>
> (Donna Williams, 1996, p. 14)

And throughout recent history, many people have been assuming autism is a set of observable behaviours. These might include rocking, flapping or lining up toys, and are invariably assumed to be seen more in boys than girls. For a long time it was assumed autism was a childhood condition, with the transition into adulthood largely ignored and much less planned for and supported.

We have come a long way from those outdated ideas of the 1940s, when Hans Asperger and Leo Kanner were studying boys with largely these stereotypical behaviours. And even though the diagnostic criteria have been updated a number of times, such as in the *Diagnostic and Statistical Manual* version 5 (DSM5) in 2013, and in the *International Classification of Diseases Manual* (ICD11), we are still a long way from matching the deficit-based diagnosis to the strength-focussed assessments that would benefit autistic identification much more.

MYTH – AUTISM IS MORE COMMON IN BOYS THAN GIRLS

This is untrue – we used to have statistics that said for every one girl there were four boys identified as autistic. That was due to the outdated stereotyped behaviours that people thought were autism. Now we know more about the inner functioning differences of autistic people, we are catching up on identifying and diagnosing the girls we missed. It is likely that soon gender will be an irrelevant consideration or area for comment.

As Donna observed, however, diagnoses are still largely dependent on observable behaviours and many autistic young people, especially but not exclusively girls, are still missed, misdiagnosed and deeply damaged by the lack of understanding and support throughout their education and future lives.

Although the DSM5 first included sensory processing difficulties, we are a long way from having those sensory differences explored beyond meeting the criteria for a diagnosis, even while autistic people are telling us how sensory processing is often at the heart of the many other difficulties they may have. We are still faced with a huge dilemma when it comes to identifying children, young people and adults who are autistic. The language of diagnosis is based on a medical model. This assumes that autism is the result of a deficit from what is considered to be 'normal.' When it is considered a disorder, it implies it is something we can 'treat' or 'fix.' Any assessment is based on what a person **cannot do and how they are significantly impaired by their condition**. The criteria uses such negative words as **abnormal, restricted** and **deficits**. This can lead to people thinking of autistic individuals as 'wrong,' 'broken' and 'abnormal.' This immediately negates the focus on what the child can do. This has seeped into our culture in schools. When we are given notice that a child has a diagnosis of autism, we can often jump to wrong conclusions or perspectives about what kind of student they are going to be and this can restrict our expectations of their potential.

> Consequently, while autistic people might be considered impaired because of their lack of spoken language, or as a result of their communication and interaction style in social situations, they are potentially further marginalised and excluded by the ways in which they are described and spoken about by others.
>
> (Woods, 2017, p. 61)

The social model applied to autism sees the impairments people experience largely caused by a lack of positive understanding, services and support. To reframe this in autism we may begin to see the 'deficits' as a difference, not a disorder.

We still have a long way to go to flip this narrative, but I am going to convince you in this book that the place we can really make a difference is in schools. Teachers have the power to change the narrative around all areas of SEND and autism and to see the strengths and potential of autistic pupils. Working together with parents, we can have good, strong ambitions for autistic pupils and help them be the best they can be.

As you read this book, you will need to know that every autistic child is different. Knowing this can help us understand some of the differences and uniqueness of each autistic child, so you can help them find the best way to achieve their potential without putting limits on what they might be able to achieve.

MYTH – WE ARE ALL A LITTLE BIT AUTISTIC

We are not. We are, however, all part of the human spectrum that is 'neurodiversity.' But autism and other conditions are a set of strengths and difficulties identified by a distinct set of criteria. All of these areas will be assessed in the diagnostic process, and the autistic person will have differences that are not the same as a neurotypical person.

Autism is a different way of thinking and processing the world and the way senses take in information about the world. Autistic people might also process internal thoughts and sensations in a different way, have strong passions and find security in repetitive behaviours. Autistic people are all different and most have many challenges when navigating the neurotypical world. The differences that autistic people usually have are in the areas of communication, social experiences, sensory processing and the way they think and learn.

The Reachout ASC Team 2020

LANGUAGE IS IMPORTANT

Even when we seek to be positive, there are debates about whether we say '**a person with autism**' or '**an autistic person**.' Once you listen to adults who have the diagnosis, you understand that **autistic** is the majority-preferred term. 'Disorder' means broken, not functioning as it should. This can do untold damage to the self-esteem of those receiving that diagnosis and impacts on the expectations others have of them. There is the same issue around using 'functioning' labels. Saying a child is 'high functioning' or 'low functioning' can lead to assumptions about the intelligence and capabilities of a child without testing these out. It dismisses the real needs of the autistic child who can manage academically and seems to manage verbally, but also leads to low expectations of the children who do not use speech or struggle to manage the sensory environment of a school (NAS, 2022).

We will use the term 'autistic' throughout the book whilst recognising that every autistic child or adult has the right to ask for the language that they prefer.

Neurodiversity is a term used to explain the diversity of human brains and how they function, acknowledging that human beings have a range of brain processing differences and need different environments to thrive. The term was coined by

Judy Singer in 1999, and she advocated for neurodiversity to be recognised along with terms such as biodiversity in the natural world.

It is a developing term, which means the word is being applied and used by different people in different ways. It will take time to embed the term and how it is used in our language. There may always be differences of opinion on how it should be used. In this book, at this time, I am sharing what I understand is the affirming vocabulary of neuro-language.

Neurotypical is a term used to describe the dominant majority of neurotype, typically relating to the academic and social norms and expectations we have of children at certain developmental stages. Our education system is designed for neurotypical development.

Neurodivergent is a term used to describe the ways of thinking, processing and developing that are different from the neurotypical norms. It can include conditions such as autism, Attention Deficit Hyperactivity Disorder (ADHD), dyslexia, dyscalculia, Developmental Coordination Disorder, Developmental Language Disorder, Tourette's Syndrome and some anxiety disorders as well as acquired brain injuries.

Please note that in this book we will be referring to autistic children. However, autism is a lifelong condition, it is the way someone IS and always will be. Please remember that our autistic children will be autistic adults, with potential to grow, to learn, to achieve, but they will always have their way of thinking, processing and experiencing the world. For this reason, you will see me refer to 'autistic people' interchangeably with 'autistic children' to remind the reader that these differences continue into adulthood. Our responsibility is not to make them 'pretend to be normal' as Donna Williams puts it, but to develop their autonomy and confidence as unique human beings.

CO-OCCURRING CONDITIONS

Brains are complex and awesome centres of processing, and autistic children can often be diagnosed with ADHD, dyslexia, epilepsy, dyspraxia, dyscalculia, Obsessive Compulsive Disorder

(OCD), Developmental Coordination Disorder, Irlen Syndrome, Ehlers-Danlos Syndrome, hypermobility, Developmental Language Disorder or any other condition. There are more children with Down's Syndrome and Cerebral Palsy being diagnosed as autistic. As teachers, this can seem overwhelming and leave us feeling ill-equipped to be specialists in all these conditions. The good news is that we don't have to be. The important thing to know when teaching an autistic or any other SEND child is to gather the information together and look at the bigger picture. Then, working with the child, the parent and with the school Special Educational Needs Co-ordinator (SENCO), or leader for inclusion, we can set the priorities based on what the child can do, and what would help them most first. The important thing is to keep reviewing the impact and progress and keeping good records of this. Where children need more than the class teacher can provide within their normal parameters of teaching (such as specific 1:1 interventions or sensory support) then the teacher will need to seek help from their school SENCO or the SENCO may seek help from other agencies.

Gordon has a diagnosis of autism and dyslexia. His teacher did some reading on both conditions and spoke to him and his mum about what he found he was able to do and what he needed the most help with. The teacher noticed that there were some common strategies that were used for both autistic and dyslexic children such as using a writing frame, a sequence of visual reminders of the key vocabulary and a letter formation visual strip, and they agreed to start with those. Implementing a process of assessing, making a plan, doing it consistently and then agreeing a date to review the progress or effectiveness enabled the teacher, the child and the parent to work together to find the best support for Gordon.

Part 1

HOW I DO THINGS DIFFERENTLY

DIFFERENTLY

The voice of autistic children

1

HOW I DO THINGS DIFFERENTLY

The voice of autistic people

COMMUNICATION

> Communication between people with and without autism
> is a two-way problem. Individuals on the spectrum may
> have communication challenges to address, but their
> typical peers and conversation partners could do more
> to meet them halfway by accepting differences in the way
> they express themselves.
>
> *(Spectrum News, accessed*
> *15 February 22)*

There is a level of mutual understanding needed between two
communication partners in order for the communication to be
understood and successful. Misinterpretation can happen on
any or both sides of the communication. Therefore, when we
are getting to know the communication of our autistic children,
we have a lot of things to take into account. These are some of
the first things to know and understand:

- Autistic children may learn language in a different way. We
  can say they have a 'spikey' language development profile
  that may not fit into the usual 'norms' by which we assess
  children's language.
- Some autistic children are gestalt language learners. This
  means they learn language through seeing whole phrases
  (gestalt means 'whole') and they repeat phrases they
  have heard connected to the context they have learned

DOI: 10.4324/9781003280064-3

them in (Prizant, 2022). So, "come on we're going to McDonald's" may be repeated at any time the child wants to go outside, because that is what the phrase means to them. This echolalia is a form of learning language that is common in autistic children. We might first notice it as repetitive words or parts of words which the child uses to comment on things or make their needs known. This can help with processing the meanings of words and phrases. Echolalia may also just sound and feel good. This is also known as a verbal 'stim.' For example, verbal stimming can be a way of communicating emotions, such as stress or excitement.

- Echolalia can also be delayed and become quite sophisticated, with whole phrases remembered in order to use them in social contexts when the autistic person can't find their own words to say.

> When I asked the teacher later, she explained that Eliza had suffered a painful splinter on the playground two years earlier. Since then, she had used the phrase "got a splinter!" whenever she felt anxious or scared.
>
> *(Prizant, 2022, p. 41)*

- Some autistic children do not develop the ability to talk. Some autistic children start to talk much later than typical children and some feel that verbal language or words are not their first language.
- Some autistic children talk very early and have an extensive vocabulary. They will astound you with their knowledge and conversation skills. They may prefer to talk to adults and may not be able to change topics or talk about things they are not familiar with. They can seem highly intelligent, but have gaps in their understanding of language or of certain social situations. Therefore, they may struggle more than we realise with the expectations that their verbal language ability means they understand everything that is said to them.

- Some of the difficulties with language can be with the **syntax** (the way language is structured, such as grammar or the correct use of pronouns), but more often there is difficulty with the **pragmatics** (the way we use language socially and flexibly), the **semantics** (the meaning of words and phrases) or the **prosody** (the rhythm of speech – tone, inflection, etc.).
- The non-verbal aspects of what is communicated, such as facial expressions and body language, might be difficult for autistic people to interpret. They may miss inferred meanings and take what is said literally. Cullen (2018, p. 6) stated:

  > Whilst it would be unreasonable to ask the neurotypical (NT) population to stop using body language in the presence of [autistic] people, it would be greatly beneficial for both parties if the NT population also express verbally what they were trying to imply or express with nonverbal communication. This would mean both parties, NT and autistic, have a better chance of understanding each other.

  > *I often got into trouble for doing just what the teacher had told me to do. The trouble was, apparently, that is not what she meant. Why can't people just say what they mean?*
  > *(Autistic adult)*

- Ever since Temple Grandin, an autistic woman, described how she thought in pictures, it has been assumed that all autistic people are more able to learn when a visual presentation of the communication is used. Whilst many autistic people do respond better to visual communication, not all do and so this needs to be checked out for the child in your class.
- Some autistic children can communicate better when given access to Additional Augmentative Communication (AAC) aids and software such as Core-word boards, Talk Mats and

Proloquo2go which would usually be recommended and supported by a Speech and Language therapist. Even those with some verbal language may find AAC makes their communication much easier.

- Eye contact is often very challenging for autistic children, and we should never insist that they look at us. For some, being able to look AND listen is difficult; for others they feel actual pain when looking at someone else's eyes. Some autistic children seem OK with giving eye contact, but when you listen to their accounts, it is something they have learned to do to 'mask' their discomfort and try to fit in.

- It is easy for us to misinterpret the communication of autistic children. Their difficulty with prosody or direct honesty can sound like rudeness.

  Teachers don't listen to me. I am very clever and clear in my mind and I know when the teacher has got something wrong so I will tell them. Instead of listening to me, they tell me off.

  (Autistic child, aged ten)

- Our cultural and racial biases need to be examined as we can misinterpret the autistic characteristics of, say, Black children as aggression or oppositional behaviour instead of understanding their autism. There has been some excellent work done by Vanessa Bobb as she works to educate people about the cultural perspectives of autism in Black and other ethnic communities.

  My children are Black. Yes Black people can be autistic too! However, in our community, as with other cultural communities, there is a problem of under-diagnosis … our voices are largely missing from research literature, conference and awareness-raising materials about autism.

  (Bobb in Carpenter et al., 2019, p. 36)

'STIMMING'

Self-stimulating or 'stimming' behaviours are an important part of what many autistic people say regulate their sensory and emotional states, as well as being a form of communication. We might see or hear a child doing something repetitively and may try to stop them doing it, but please first ask yourself what harm they are doing? Self-stimulating behaviours are connected to sensory feedback and emotional regulation, and the repetitive nature of behaviours such as rocking provide comfort and even joy. Most human beings stim. Do you twiddle your hair or bite your fingernails? Do you flick a pen or tap your foot? All these things are the brain's way of calming down or alerting the person to be able to cope, pay attention or feel safe. Therefore, we should not try to 'get rid' of the stimming, unless the stim is harmful, such as biting themselves or picking at their skin, when we should gently try to address the underlying cause and try to find a replacement activity that helps them feel safe and comforted.

Stims can be physical, sensory or verbal and letting the child do what helps them regulate will be an important part of their support. In a primary school there should not be issues around being seen to be different if the culture of the school is already accepting and purposefully promoting acceptance of people in all their differences.

> *I use noises and humming to block out the noises in the background that hurt my ears. Sometimes it gets so bad that I scream, it shuts out the pain of those other noises.*
>
> *(Autistic child, aged nine)*

> *I make noises when I am happy and thinking about my stories and songs that I love. This can be in the middle of a lesson when the urge to sing is stronger than the effort I need to be quiet in the lesson.*
>
> *(Autistic child, aged ten)*

Not everyone understands when I am self-stimulating, my way of doing this is by walking around the classroom, which not all members of staff allow me to do. One in particular told me it was rude.

(Autistic child, Spectrum Gaming)

2

SOCIAL INTERACTION

All communication is social by its definition. What we often mean by social interaction is the making of friends and positive relationships, playing with others and doing activities together with mutual engagement and pleasure.

MYTH – AUTISTIC CHILDREN ARE ANTI-SOCIAL OR DON'T WANT FRIENDS

This is not true. Some autistic children withdraw from social situations because they are overwhelming (see Hilary's account below), they are too unstructured or they have had negative experiences before that have destroyed their confidence. Most autistic children do want to have friends, but they want friends who will accept them for who they are, who will allow them to be themselves and who are kind. It's sad that this kind of friend is so elusive for so many autistic children and so many of them experience serious bullying.

When we say that autistic children have social difficulties it is often because we don't understand their experience of social situations. Dr Damian Milton (2018) has developed the Double Empathy Theory which explains that whilst it is true that autistic people struggle to understand social cues, social meanings and what might be expected of them socially, it is also true that other people don't understand the social cues, social meanings and attempts at interacting from the autistic person's point of view. This can be incredibly useful as we work to support

DOI: 10.4324/9781003280064-4

autistic children and you will see this theory threading through the advice we give.

Anna loved going to nursery. Her favourite things there were the dressing up clothes. She would dress up as her favourite Disney characters and then try to get the other children to play along with her. But this is when the problems happened. Anna couldn't find the words to say "do you want to play with me?" so she would stand alongside the other children hoping they would get the message. When they didn't she would get frustrated and hit them on the arm. What she was really saying is, "why didn't you know I want you to play with me."

Peter Vermueluen (2012) explains how the autistic brain functions in understanding the world, communication and interactions, often finding pulling all the information together in its context quite difficult. The context of our communication impacts on what we are trying to communicate and what we understand from other people's communication to us. The difficulty for autistic children is that they may have a different perspective on experiences due to having had some past negative social experiences. It could take longer to find what they are needing in their memory and by the time they have worked it out, the context and situation has moved on and what they were going to do or say is no longer relevant. Even some autistic adults say that they often have no idea about what is going on in a social situation, they feel extremely vulnerable and anxious, and that other people are judging them unkindly. Autistic children can be vulnerable to being taken advantage of by others who think it is fun to make the autistic child do things they shouldn't on the fake promise of being their friend. A lot of bullying can start this way and the danger for autistic children is that they may not know they are even being bullied until things get very seriously out of hand.

Unpredictability is a huge stress for many autistic children. It is why they like routine, order, to control things and to know exactly what is happening. Social situations, by their very nature, are full of unpredictable events, not knowing what someone wants, what their mood is or where the conversation is going. Playtimes and lunchtimes, when usually neurotypical children are relaxing and being refreshed ready for the next lesson, are an opposite experience for many autistic children.

> *My close, close friends understand because I've known them for a while, but apart from that I get called names on a daily basis and I can't tell anyone. I love my mum and dad and never want to stress them more than I already am.*
> *(Autistic child, Spectrum Gaming)*

ACCOUNT FROM ONE AUTISTIC PERSON:

On a one to one, there is, well, one interaction. When another joins in then there are six potential interactions, because there is each person interacting with each of the other two so that is three interactions, plus each person's interaction with the other two, when the other two act as one in some way, e.g., opinion, agreement, etc. So six in total.

Now, there is an easy way to work out the number of interactions for a given number of people. If there are three people then we simply need to multiply three by two by one = six. This is written as 3! The exclamation mark is known as a factorial sign. So then one more person joins ... now there are 4! potential interactions which = 4×3×2×1 = 24. This may possibly be about my limit but mostly if I am one of the four people, but it's still a big challenge because now I am feeling all the unspoken undercurrents that 24 potential interactions produces. Throw into this several different personality types and possible tension between two or more of the people and it's possible to see how a storm can quickly brew of unspoken emotions, thoughts, etc.

However, I generally hang on in there, but know I'll pay the price with exhaustion and several recovery days where I avoid as much social interaction as possible. (Just a note to add that I do of course sometimes 'do' social groups with friends I know well or am comfortable with, as a trusted group of friends makes a huge difference, as does having a focus such as having a meal with friends and because I am already familiar with the types of interactions which happen and the whole experience is less exhausting. The better I know people in the group, the easier it is, generally. I still don't 'do' social events and social groups often though.)

Now, a fifth person comes along, and this basically explodes in my head. 5! potential interactions, that is $5 \times 4 \times 3 \times 2 \times 1 = 120$ undercurrents which are cross-firing what is actually being said ... add in a few looks, glances, smiles, frowns, tones of voice, buttings in, and there you have it, I'm gone, looking for the kettle and a quiet corner and maybe one person I know well enough to have a nice quiet brew with or better still friends' cat(s) who totally understand and retreated to quiet corners already. Add one more person ... and now the potential number of interactions rises exponentially ... 6! That's $6 \times 5 \times 4 \times 3 \times 2 \times 1 = 720$. Seven people, 7! = $7 \times 720 = 5{,}040$ potential interactions.

What generally happens though, is that the limit of a useful group is probably four, though three is in my opinion better still. At five, usually the quieter people give way to the more verbal, and melt into the background either gratefully or in some frustration. So this curbs the actual number of interactions, but not by much due to the unspoken emotions which flow like wifi among the group. I have come to realise that it must be an acute awareness of these ridiculous number of interactions, with equal awareness

> *of the accompanying undercurrents that make the whole group experience feel to me as if I were being slapped in the face every nanosecond. The huge difference between a social group of say five people and a group which has gathered for a specific focus on say a film or lecture or even in some sense to play some sort of game or sport, is that if there is one focus that the group has then immediately it is in reality a one to one situation, almost, with each person in the group interacting mainly on the focus, and all five people also acting as one person interacting with the focus.*
> *(Hilary Forbes, autistic maths teacher)*

As Hilary pointed out, social interactions are often exhausting for autistic people. The effort and energy needed to manage in these situations take it out of them and there are often other stresses they are trying to manage whilst social situations are going on, such as sensory stress. Some autistic children develop serious anxiety and mental ill health, even in primary school because there are too many social demands and no rest from them. **Autistic burnout** is a result. Sadly, even though this is more common in teenagers, the roots often begin in primary school.

MASKING

There will be times in your teaching career when you will hear from parents that their child is having meltdowns at home almost every day after school and they will want to know what is happening at school to cause these. However, to your eyes there will not be a problem at school. The child seems a little quiet perhaps, but they are well behaved in class and have friends to play with at playtimes. To you they are 'fine in school' and therefore it is easy to assume that the problem is that the parents are doing something wrong. This is a common problem for autistic children who have learned early on to **mask** their difficulties and autistic characteristics. It's more than just trying to fit in. It's often driven by huge anxiety and rejection sensitivity that causes panic and trauma at the hint of getting anything wrong, or being 'found out.' If undetected this strategy can seem to be working far into the primary years. But often it begins to unravel in the pre-teen years as the other children start to develop socially more complex relationships and the autistic child is left floundering. **Masking** is more than trying to fit in; it is a denial of their own identity and character, so much so that the autistic child is very vulnerable to disassociating from themselves and taking on the character and personality of others. The stress of holding this all in and keeping up the act at school all day becomes intolerable by the time the child reaches their safe place at home. And then the emotional explosion happens.

Imagine it like a bottle of cola that has been shaken up all through the day and the child has just managed not to let the lid blow off. But the lid will blow once the pressure has got too much. We can do a lot to ease that pressure gently throughout the day at school.

DOI: 10.4324/9781003280064-5

The thing about **masking** is not to underestimate the toll it takes on the autistic child. The parents of the majority of autistic children I know that have had mental ill health, severe anxiety and been unable to attend school have at some time been told "they are fine in school." And as teachers, it will seem like they are. Internalising the distress is a huge effort for autistic children and not being believed, being afraid of being told off and just not knowing how to be themselves will start to unravel in some way eventually. It is too easy to think it is the parents being too anxious and that going on a parenting course will sort it out. I even know a wonderful parent who runs the parenting courses for her local authority who was told she would not get help for her child unless she went and did the parenting course!

Therefore, if a parent says their child is having meltdowns at home, please believe them and agree to investigate together.

> *I masked because I was scared of getting in trouble for being cheeky, so I didn't say what I really wanted to say.*
> *(Hope, aged ten)*

What Hope told me was that she hasn't been to school for two years. Her teachers told her off, would not allow her to have her sensory breaks and said she was putting it on. This autistic child is bright, talented and wants to be in a school where she is understood, safe and allowed to be herself, but is currently exhausted and unable to find a school where she feels able to.

> *Please listen to the parents and not brush them off, or assume that the parent is exaggerating or anxious. A child may mask at school as they don't feel safe enough to be themselves. They may be being 'fine' and 'good' because they don't want to be seen as different, are unable to express needs, in sensory overload or something else. The pressure on the entire family when schools don't listen is destructive and causes trauma.*
> *(Emma, Hope's mum)*

4

THE AUTISTIC SENSORY EXPERIENCE

All the information we take in about the world around us comes in via our senses.

From getting out of bed to going to sleep, your brain is constantly taking in and assessing sensory information. We cannot function without our brains knowing what is going on, sending messages to our muscles and joints to make us move, to avoid things that are dangerous or uncertain and to manage self-care and keep safe. We mostly do all these things without thinking. We don't think about how to walk once we have mastered the skill as a child; our brain develops its motor memory and we just walk. It's much more complex than that, but what we need to know as teachers is that the sensory processing of our autistic pupils is fundamental to everything else ... their access to everyday environments, their communication, their social interactions, their emotions and their thinking and learning.

Autistic people are telling us that the sensory experiences they have are largely dependent on the environments we have created and also the internal sensations and motivations they have. Therefore, some environments are overwhelming and sensory 'hell' for autistic children, such as a classroom that has strip lighting or a dining hall that smells strongly of different foods every day, and the playground full of noisy, moving (and screaming) children. Many behaviours we see are the autistic person either trying to cope with the sensory 'hell' or a way of seeking sensory comfort and regulation internally. Sensory joy is a thing too, and we should not attempt to stop children doing a sensory activity that they are using to cope, manage or seek

DOI: 10.4324/9781003280064-6

their happy place. (These could be activities such as flapping, bouncing or cuddling a favourite toy.)

> As a pre-teen, I remember being obsessed with the concept of 'normal.' I distinctly remember comparing myself to my classmates and being sure that I was the odd one out. Over time I grew to realise that 'normal' is a harmful myth, and that all the things that made me 'stand out' were the things that made me who I am. I grew to celebrate being autistic.
>
> *(Dean Beadle, autistic adult)*

The reality for our autistic children in school is that the environment, the lessons and all the demands of the day can be perceived differently through their senses. They may have a much smaller window of tolerance than other children in some sensory systems. The level of stress at any time impacts on the way the autistic child reacts to a sensory event, from rage and meltdown when highly stressed, to quiet withdrawal or internalised anxiety.

> I can tell you the name and model of every aeroplane that flies over our school because I know the different engine sounds. Being in a classroom is like torture. I can hear absolutely everything in my classroom and the three classrooms around us. I spend the whole lesson trying to concentrate on the teacher's voice and it is exhausting. I am always anxious about what the other kids are going to do or say, which means I am fighting that too. I go home and I have to go to bed, with my earphones in to recover. The thing is, that listening to music helps. But the teacher said I can't listen to music in class.
>
> *(Autistic child, 2017)*

It will help us to understand that there are eight sensory systems. These can all be **hypo-**, that is, **under-sensitive**, which means that the brain does not receive enough sensory feedback or stimulation and may either ignore or seek out more sensory input. This can be seen in children who are constantly seeking movement for example. Often it is much less notice-able, such as when a child doesn't respond to someone talking to them or seems to be zoning out of what is going on around them. The sensory systems can also be **hyper-**, that is, **over-sensitive**, which means that the brain is receiving too much information and finds it hard to cope or manage it. It can be anything from clothing to noise and smells – the school envi-ronment is a hotbed of overwhelming sensory experiences. The sensory systems can be a mixture of over- and under-sensitive in any child and environmental conditions, anxiety and tiredness can further complicate the situation, e.g., not just increase sensitivity, but also make processing information more challenging. It is not uncommon for the sensitivity to change throughout the day, for example, when a child might be tired in the afternoon.

This is only a general overview of some of the sensory pro-cessing experiences we can find in autistic children.

1. **Sight** – the visual system includes what we see and how we interpret all the parts of what we see to make a whole pic-ture. Our brains interpret the sights and put them together with the relevant other sensory signals (such as sounds) to help us interpret the world around us. In school we assume children are using their sight to refer to the relevant infor-mation, follow and track our teaching, read and write and interact with the environment.

   - Autistic children can be face-blind (a small percentage but worth checking), colour-blind, have Irlen Syndrome (requiring coloured lenses to see clearly) or fractured visual perception.
   - They may only be able to focus on certain narrow or specific details or be easily distracted by the huge amounts of movement, displays, colours, light levels and visual changes in school.
   - They may have an excellent visual memory that helps them learn, and be a strong visual learner.

- Some autistic children love the visual excitement of something flapping in front of their eyes, such as a straw.
- Some might flick the lights on and off, or hide in dark places.

> When his teacher took all the toys, boxes and posters away from around the whiteboard, Khan, aged six, could focus on the lesson much more easily. Before that he was so fascinated by looking at the cuddly toys on the top of the board that he couldn't listen to the lessons at all.

2. **Hearing** - autistic children are often very sensitive to sound.

- The teacher's tone of voice, another adult speaking at the same time and noise from the road outside or the other classrooms can have a strong impact on the autistic child being able to learn in your class.
- The more voices there are to switch attention to, the harder it is to manage conversations and tune into what is important.
- Unexpected noises, loud or sudden noises and noises with certain tones can all be different triggers.
- Autistic children can also have auditory processing disorder and have hearing disabilities.

> Holly was so afraid of the school bell that she would get increasingly distressed towards the end of each lesson. She constantly asked the teacher when the lesson would end and would spend the last ten minutes of every lesson holding her ears, and often crying. The head teacher decided to stop using a bell for the end of lessons throughout the

school, and Holly was able to manage the whole school day better. Other children then started to say how they were relieved the bell wasn't there anymore.

3. **Smell** – we can underestimate the number of smells in a classroom. Many of us desensitise to familiar smells but many autistic children may not.

   - The food being cooked in the kitchen, your perfume, the sweaty bodies of year 6 after PE, the carpet or school toilets can be overwhelming and distressing for autistic children.
   - Other autistic children may have a poor sense of smell and cannot tell when they have body odour or when something is burning. This can also impact on the range of foods that they will eat. They may seek out strong smells and enjoy strong flavours.

I once had a child say to me "I can't work with you today, you stink." And I realised that I had put perfumed deodorant on that day. He was right and we managed to sit far enough apart for that visit to manage the session I had come to do. But I remembered to wear my unperfumed deodorant every time after that.

4. **Taste** – school snack and lunch times can be so overwhelming for autistic children, and so can food-based lessons. Some children may eat non-food items to stimulate their senses (we call that Pica).

   - They may have a limited palate of foods they can manage to eat without making their senses scream, or they may have the need to control the order and pace at which they eat.

- Texture, smell and taste work together, but in schools, as a class teacher you may not see the needs your autistic child has because you are not with them at lunch times. For some, the combined sensory experience of eating in front of others in the noisy hall and the demands to hurry up or eat something in a different order can be very distressing. There is a strong case for making sure that lunch time supervisors have some autism training.

> *Being able to eat my lunch in a quiet space with two of my friends makes all the difference to my school life.*
>
> *(Autistic child, aged nine)*

5. **Touch** - our skin is our biggest organ and has many nerve endings that are sensitive to touch. We often explore the world through touch, and hyper-sensitivity to textures and objects in the environment like chairs and the carpet can be common. Under-sensitivity to touch means the person can seem clumsy or fidgety, often seeking to touch and handle things to try and register them.

   - Some autistic people say that a light touch can feel like hot pins attacking their skin, or not be registered at all. Autistic children may hate the unpredictability of people being near them, or being in crowded places.
   - Some autistic children can't stand touching certain textures, or textures that are mixed together (be aware of that in your early years sensory play tray).
   - Some can't stand the labels on clothing or the seam in their socks, or wearing shoes.
   - Some autistic children seek out touch, wanting to hug people or stroke lots of things in the classroom. They may have favourite cuddly toys or a piece of fabric they need for sensory comfort.

- Some may strip off their clothing or not be able to cope with different temperatures or weather.
- Some develop a fear of touching things, or a need to do repetitive actions that help them ground themselves in an intolerable environment.

Corina couldn't line up without screaming. It turned out she was super sensitive to being touched and being too near people made it worse as she was additionally anxious about not knowing who would touch her and when. It was quite simple to help her. She was allowed to join the line last and at the back. She could control the space between her and the other children, and no-one needed to notice or make a comment, so she did not feel singled out.

---

6. **Vestibular (balance)** – this is our sense of movement and balance. The vestibular sense is important for coordination and organisation. We use it to support our tracking, e.g., looking up from a desk to the board and back again. It tells us if we are moving, and if so whether fast or slow, up or down, in a straight line or in different directions, and helps us keep our balance when our body is in a precarious position.

- Autistic children may have poor balance and struggle with planning the speed and coordination of movements.
- They may be over-sensitive and have motion sickness, which they may not be able to explain to you (it is perhaps just their normal state) and will impact on the way they move around the classroom and school, and make PE very challenging.
- They may have excellent balance and be able to climb any available obstacle.

- They may seek out movement to help regulate their sensory system – which may include rocking, running around or climbing high to satisfy that need.

Adam could not sit still and was always swinging on his chair and would get up after only a few minutes in his seat. We provided him with regular movement breaks with lots of movements in different directions – simply a game of chase would help at break times and other children were willing to play this with him.

---

7. **Proprioception (body and spatial awareness)** – people usually don't have an over-sensitive proprioception sensory system, but this sensory system can be under-sensitive. This body awareness is centred in your muscles and joints, giving the brain feedback as to where you are, planning movements and reactions. Dyspraxia, or Developmental Coordination Disorder (DCD) as it is now called, is closely related to poor proprioception.

   - An autistic child may be very fidgety, unable to regulate their body to stay still comfortably. The brain is just not receiving enough feedback and sends strong requests for more movement so it can register where the body is and if it is safe.
   - They may be sluggish, always leaning on walls and people to feel grounded and find it difficult to manage in their own space. This can also indicate poor vestibular processing.
   - Autistic children with under-sensitive proprioception may need support in their seating and movement breaks to develop body awareness and may need to fiddle to gain the feedback from their body that the brain needs.

- Anxiety and concentration may be improved by proprioceptive exercises or activities.

Harry was only five when his mum attended a training session I did about the sensory systems. The next time I saw her she said how learning about proprioception had changed their lives. Instead of trying to get him to calm down to get ready for bedtime (it hadn't been working) they realised he was seeking this deep pressure and movement in his body. They started giving him a rough and tumble time with lots of deep hugs, wrapping him up and squashing him with cushions before bedtime. He then started to sleep really well.

I disliked PE to an extent: I remember getting very frustrated at being unable to throw, catch or kick a football particularly well. I seemed to have problems with balance and hand-eye coordination and did not like the feel of the ball, bat, or racket being used.

(Jackson, aged 21, reflecting on his
primary school experience)

8. **Interoception (internal sensations)** – this is one of the most important breakthroughs in our understanding of the sensory systems. Interoception regulates our internal sensations like knowing when we need to go to the toilet, when we are hungry, feeling pain, sickness, tiredness and the like. It is also connected to our emotions and our ability to recognise when we are feeling an emotion.

- Toileting, eating and sleep difficulties are common in autistic children and it is important to talk to parents about this.
- Emotions are complex events. Thoughts, body sensations and reactions (such as flight, fight or freeze) are felt internally and not always registered by the brain.

Not connecting to emotional sensations and being unable to interpret them (and therefore communicate how they are feeling) is called **alexithymia**.

- Some autistic children are over-sensitive to emotions. This means they feel them in their bodies as huge reactions. Sadly, they are often dismissed as over-reacting.

Dan was autistic and anxious most of the time. It prevented him from doing anything without absolute control or certainty. Working with him to explore their sensory systems, we realised that he interpreted all his internal emotional signals as anxiety, and he particularly had a delay of two days to four weeks before his brain registered his emotions. That meant it was difficult for him to say what was worrying at the time, and when he did work it out, it was dismissed as being in the past. When I worked with him on naming and recognising other emotions, he began to slowly start to recognise when he was feeling a range of emotions that he could communicate to trusted others. We also developed vocabulary that was meaningful to him; for Dan it was colours.

Sensory assessments can be done by a therapist who is sensory integration trained. Considering that sensory differences are part of the autism diagnostic criteria, it is sad that not all autistic children receive an assessment as part of their diagnosis, much as they should receive a speech and language assessment (NICE, 2017). If that is not immediately possible, work with parents and with what you can easily find out about the child. There are some links in the Resources chapter at the back of this book.

All autistic children are unique in how their sensory systems work and function, and an individual approach can be supported in a mainstream classroom. The sensory systems are complex as the senses also integrate and work together. Difficulties with proprioception, vestibular and touch perception lead into potential difficulties with planning, sequencing and organising movement. Sight and balance are integral to movement and taste, smell and touch also work closely together to help us make sense of our world and function within it. There is also a strong link between sensory soothing and managing anxiety, so we must be very careful not to stop or dismiss an autistic child's rocking, fiddling or doodling, for example. Being told to stop and made to feel wrong does harm to the child. It internalises their distress and causes long-term anxiety and mental ill health (Verhulst et al., 2022).

Part 2

TEACHING AUTISTIC CHILDREN
Practical strategies

5

GETTING IT RIGHT FROM THE START

I used to love a new school year. I loved getting my classroom looking clean and fresh, putting up welcoming displays and creating seating plans, and would be looking forward to getting to know a new set of lovely children whom I was sure I would love and have a great year with. A new school year is an excellent time to reflect on our teaching experience and put into effect new things and approaches to build on what we have learned. We know the reality of how pressures, planning, curriculum demands and teaching observations build up over the year. To have to do extra work for one or more Special Educational Needs and Disabilities (SEND) children can seem quite daunting, especially if you are fearful of getting it wrong, or you feel that you tried things already with previous pupils and they didn't work. At the heart of every teacher I have supported, there is the desire to help the child. This is where we can start from, and the aspects to focus on first are what we know and what has gone well already.

GETTING THE RELATIONSHIP WITH THE PARENTS RIGHT

The autistic child is very likely to be feeling anxious about meeting a new teacher and being in a new classroom. You could be anxious to get this year right for them and be wondering what might work best. The key to this is to focus first on getting to know the child and their parents or carers. If the child has a teaching assistant 1:1, then they need to be involved in this from the start, as do any general class teaching assistants. This relationship will build the support and development around the child to have a successful year with you, and to pass all that you learn on to the next teacher.

DOI: 10.4324/9781003280064-8

- Discuss with the Special Educational Needs Co-ordinator (SENCO) in your school what involvement there has been with the family up to now. Don't be put off by past negative or difficult situations and agree with the SENCO on how you might lead the relationship with parents while the child is in your class. The SEND Code of Practice (2014) states that all teachers are responsible for all children in their class. It is their responsibility to listen to the child, whose voice and needs should be at the heart of all programmes, decisions and support, and work with the family and other professionals.

- Know what the Graduated Approach (SEND Code of Practice 2014) is, and plan to build a robust system of assess, plan, implement and review whatever support the child may need. You will need to cover not only **cognition and learning** needs, but also the other areas outlined in the SEND Code of Practice. These are **sensory and physical** needs, **communication and interaction** needs (which need to take into account the communication style of your autistic pupil) and **social, emotional and mental health** (which should support the child's anxiety, social relationships and emotional regulation). Much of what we learn will be from interacting with and observing the child, but do try to look for what they can do, what they are interested in and what you can do that has been proven to work first and foremost. Then we can build up from those things.

- Set up the first meeting with the parents. Try to make this informal and notify them of the agenda before the meeting, which gives them time to prepare and understand what the meeting is about. Reassure them that you are wanting to get to know their child and start off on the right track. It is worth considering that some parents may also be autistic and good, structured communication will be helpful and necessary for them too.

- Set dates for the follow up meeting where you can all review what progress or continuing barriers there are for the child. You may need to agree a communication structure with parents, who will want to know how each day has gone, especially if their child is one who 'keeps the lid on all day' and then expresses all their frustration, anxiety and stress at home. We often use a **visual home-school sheet** with symbols or pictures of the activities, space to write about emotions of the day and comments on what has been achieved and what has been difficult. They are quick and easy to fill in for a busy teacher or teaching assistant and give parents something to go through with their child, especially those who can't find words to tell their parents about the day. For some parents it may seem that the child is having a very negative day, all day, every day ... but with regulation times throughout the day and supporting the child to review the day visually, we can record what has been successful and enjoyable for them. Be careful not to impose your view on whether an activity was OK for the child; we should acknowledge that even successful activities can be draining and overwhelming for an autistic child.

- The strengths, interests and sensory needs of the child can be collected through a visual map too. Figures 5.1 and 5.2

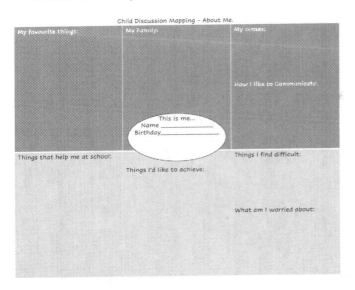

Figure 5.1 Child discussion mat.

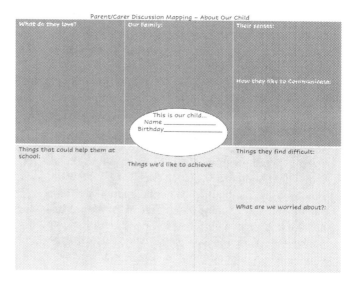

Figure 5.2 Parent/carer discussion mat.

show some examples of a guided conversation with the parents and one to use with the child (which can be illustrated through pictures, drawings and symbols if they make the communication easier for the child).

They should have known everything about me that we knew, as me and my parents told them multiple times.
                                    (Autistic child, Spectrum Gaming)

6

THE CLASSROOM ENVIRONMENT

Autism + environment = outcomes.

(Dr Luke Beardon, 2019, p. 11)

THE CLASSROOM LAYOUT – EARLY YEARS

In the early years the classroom layout is busy. There is a lot of equipment set out each day and a lot of sensory experiences on offer. There is nothing wrong with this, but we have to understand that for a young autistic child this can be very overwhelming. If you sit on the floor of your early years classroom you will see things from the child's eye view and can maybe see where some adjustments can be made.

- Is there a clear route to where you might want to go?
- Is there anything that could be unpredictable? (Even stationary toys and equipment might fall or be moved and look different each day.)
- Is there anything the child likes; can you see it from where you are?
- What is the lighting like; is it too bright or too dull in different areas?
- Are there strong smells of the classroom or nearby toilets?
- Is the thing the child likes too near a noisy activity?

For an autistic child navigating your environment, we add in a whole set of other children, moving around, doing what they want to do, talking, calling, moving things and having their own agendas. The other children are highly unpredictable and may take up space where you want to go or to be. There are huge adults who keep talking to you, telling you things you can't

DOI: 10.4324/9781003280064-9

process fast enough or just can't comply with, because it's too difficult to move when all this chaos is going on. There are loud noises, sudden temperature changes, sudden demands and so much unpredictability.

> To me the outside world is a totally baffling incomprehensible mayhem which terrifies me. It is a meaningless mass of sights and sounds, noises and movements, coming from nowhere, going nowhere.
>
> (Ros Blackburn, 2021)

I have observed many autistic children who seem lost in the early years classroom; often they are reluctant to come inside, and parents can have huge difficulty getting them into school. You may think that once they are inside and parents have left, they seem to settle down and be okay. However, if you watch carefully, you might see their masking and coping skills that limit what they interact with and engage with throughout the day. These can include only going to one play area that they feel they can cope with, withdrawing and 'flitting' between areas and not really engaging with play in any area or withdrawing into fantasy scenarios where they take on a role that is more confident, in control and predictable.

Other autistic children struggle visibly from the start. This may be seen in reluctance, refusal, aggression, self-harm and meltdown in the classroom on a daily basis.

Elias joined the reception class after a difficult year in nursery. He stayed in one place at the computer table most of the day. He would seem to have a huge meltdown if staff tried to get him to let others have a go with the computer or stop the game he was playing in order to come to the carpet or get ready for going out to play. I watched him navigate the reception classroom. He kept looking around him with a look of terror in his eyes. When another child came near him he would flinch and push them away so they wouldn't touch him. When the song was put on the board to signify tidy up time, he would put his hands on his ears and start to rock. Elias was in an environment that terrified him, and his only solace was the computer games that helped him stay as calm as he could.

- **Simplify the layout**. Think about putting fewer activities out each day and increase the space between each activity. One teacher I know zoned each area with coloured paper on the walls so children could easily recognise each area and navigate the room by this visual clue. Have quiet spaces for children to hide away from the sensory stimulation for a while and it may be a good idea to have one of these near the carpet space so that they can still listen to a story or song time without having to feel overwhelmed.
- **Less visual content around the classroom, including displays**. Autistic children are already having to process so much sensory information that being in a too busy, too bright environment with lots of things hanging from the ceiling can lead to great distress. You can still have your castle-, doctors- or pirate ship-themed areas, but if you concentrate the display to one area, it makes it visually clear what the area is about. The research on calmer classroom displays is compelling but inconclusive; however, there is a more significant impact of a low-impact display area for autistic children (Hanley et al., 2017).
- **Have a special interest area for the autistic child with two of everything**. Autistic children can learn through their special interests and often have great joy in play or learning with these. Let them know they have an area they can go to that is safe and calm for them. Add sensory objects they like, and it will be an oasis. Other children can go there too but make it clear it is a calm space. Sharing might be difficult, so having at least two of everything might help the

autistic child manage other children playing with the toys they like best.

Elias's reception class teacher spent time changing the environment to make it calmer and simpler. He did this gradually and involved Elias to show him what he was doing so that there were no unexpected changes. Displays were made simpler and lots of equipment that had been out on tables and on top of cupboards was put away, in accessible labelled boxes. He gave Elias some control and choices around the classroom and built up the communication visual talk mats around the activities. Teaching assistants were assigned to spend some time with Elias each day taking some dinosaurs (his favourite things) to visit each of the areas where another dinosaur had been hidden, and find out what could be done there, taking the lead from Elias's curiosity. Staff modelled and pointed to the vocabulary mats and other children would join them and invite Elias to play with them. He could say yes or no using the mats. Gradually he started to say yes more, and the teaching assistants could draw back a little. Elias needed other support but these first steps allowed him to access the environment, routines and activities much more calmly.

THE CLASSROOM LAYOUT – LOWER PRIMARY CLASSROOMS

Similarly, a primary classroom can be an overwhelming environment. The change is often in the number of tables and chairs, and the amount of time that children are expected to be sitting at those tables and chairs. In classrooms for the younger children, there is often a carpet area where they are expected to sit cross-legged and listen for maybe 20-30 minutes. The anxiety about where to sit and the sensory discomfort or distraction during carpet time can be a barrier to the autistic child joining in with the activities there. It is common for autistic children to struggle with that time because we haven't made it clear why they are there or how long they will be there for, and we don't make any adaptations for those children with sensory difficulties in that enclosed and overwhelming mini environment.

The size of the classroom, the position of the windows, and the number of children in the class are beyond our control; however, there are many things we can still do to make this environment an autism-friendly environment for autistic children.

- **Consider the layout.** You will of course need to have enough tables and chairs for all the children in your class as well as a base for yourself, storage and display. Children could be packed in close together and so it makes sense for there to be a minimalistic approach to how much other equipment and 'stuff' there is in the classroom. Ask if cupboards or lockers can be outside the classroom, and try not to have coats, bags and lunch boxes on open shelves that distract the visual line of the children.
- Have a clear space around the whiteboard and between display boards so that there is a clear visual indication of what to look at and less chance children will be distracted.
- Check light levels and, if possible, get rid of flickering tube lights (autistic children can be very sensitive to these – imagine sitting in a strobe light all day).
- A clear route to their chair, a space they can personalise, somewhere the light is adjustable and a nearby calm space to escape to if needed can be very helpful and enable them to feel safe in your classroom.
- **Carpet space.** Autistic children can be overwhelmed by the space, so a predictable spot for them to sit in should always be available. You can mark this with a carpet square, cushion or chair for the child to sit on. Take into account the amount of space they need between them and other children, as young children can easily bump into each other, reach out, touch, fiddle and fidget.
- When autistic children just cannot cope with the carpet space and time, then introduce a space near the carpet, or a favoured activity on a nearby table so that they can listen in. I once knew a child who learned all his phonics in this way. By not demanding he sit down and by allowing him to

play with his dinosaurs, the teacher ensured he was able to listen to every word being taught and he became the first to know all his phonic sounds in that class.

- **Displays and visual reminders**. If you think about a child who notices everything in their environment or those who can't visually focus easily, we can understand how the visual 'noise' of lots of busy displays can be more of a hindrance than a help. Lowering the amount of display and being clear what and where things are in the classroom can reduce anxiety and make the environment easier to work in for many children.
- I have seen some helpful flipbooks on tables where children learn to flip the pages to the one that is relevant to that lesson and the visual reminders are easier to access that way rather than scanning the walls for the information.
- Try to have at least one clear wall and invite any children who like to sit near it to do so.

Sensory adaptations can have a huge impact. There are lots of small sensory changes you can make that reduce the triggers and overload, especially for autistic children.

- Blinds (solid ones are preferable to vertical ones that move in the breeze) on windows enable you to control the light levels.
- Putting things away in cupboards and labelling the cupboard doors enables children to know where things are without having to be visually overwhelmed.
- Rubber stoppers on the chair and table legs reduce scraping noises.
- Closing the door reduces background noise.
- Not having PE just before or after lunch can reduce smell overload. Also consider lower intensity options during PE, or, for some, higher intensity and not too much sitting and waiting!
- Having a calm or sensory corner in your class can give an autistic child a place to feel safe and to regulate rather than having to go out of class or become more distressed.

- Be aware of what you wear, too – check with the child that your clothes are not too bright or your perfume/deodorant isn't causing them sensory pain.

ADDITIONAL ENVIRONMENT ADAPTATIONS IN UPPER PRIMARY CLASSROOMS

In the upper primary years (ages 7–11), in many educational settings, children are expected to sit and listen for much longer periods of time and have much less opportunity for movement and play. **The sensory needs of autistic pupils may not diminish; in fact, they may be more important due to the demands of the curriculum and social interactions as they grow older.** The expectations on the children to be more independent and organised, the increased vocabulary and the interpretation demands in the curriculum may mean that autistic pupils can benefit from support that teachers may think they have 'grown out of.' Many autistic pupils do grow and learn, they develop their academic skills and can often have areas of exceptional ability. Other autistic pupils may have learning disabilities such as dyslexia or dyscalculia which have not been picked up on. It can be easy to explain everything as being due to their being autistic. Therefore, rather than assuming they may have grown out of supports like visual timetables, seating arrangements and calm areas, we can instead adapt these environmental supports to suit the growing needs and demands of the individual autistic pupil.

> Levels of sensitivity to environmental factors vary between individuals and within the same individual over time, so that the presentation of autism is ever changing. A person's neurological type, however, remains constant, and being autistic is a lifelong identity.
>
> *(Leatherland in Beardon, 2019, p. 16)*

- **Consider the layout.** As children grow bigger, classrooms can get more crowded with the larger furniture and space needed by each child. Seating arrangements can be rows, groups or individual tables and thinking about how you can communicate best with all the children in your class will help you think about the layout that may suit them.

- Let them contribute to where they sit and how to organise the equipment and visual prompts they might need. Check that they have a safe and calm place to go to if they are overwhelmed (this is often in the classroom, but may be a special place in another part of the school; for example, one child had a chair by the fish tank in the school reception which was his regulation place.)

- For autistic pupils and other pupils, classroom displays can still cause visual overload well into the school year and throughout their upper primary years, therefore thinking about alternative ways of prompting in different lessons might be more effective.

- Give autistic (and maybe all) children the option to use a three-sided foldable privacy screen when they are working and want to shut out the distractions around them.

- The strategy ideas from lower primary can often be needed right through the primary years. **If it is working, please don't assume they don't need it any more**.

- When autistic children start puberty as they do in the upper primary years, their sensory sensitives can become more intense and acute. Unexpected changes and new activities can lower the ability to tolerate sensory experiences and so keeping this in mind and making sure there is a sensory safe place for your autistic pupils, whatever the class is doing, will be very helpful to them.

Freshfield Primary School in Formby, Merseyside worked on making all their classrooms as inclusive as possible. The layout of the classrooms and the meaningful use of adults means needs are largely being met within the classroom itself. This meant less withdrawal for interventions which creates safety and belonging for children with additional needs. Using a palette of soft browns, greens and creams, they used hessian to back display boards and left clear spaces between display boards. There are plain walls and calm 'regulation stations' in every classroom which any of the children can go to if they are needing a bit of emotional regulation time. Teachers, children, and parents have commented on how much calmer the school space feels and teachers are finding that not having to put so much effort into constantly creating displays is freeing up their time to do other things they want to do for the children.

Figure 6.1 One of the redesigned autism-friendly classrooms at Freshfield Primary School, Formby

The last word on this must go to the autistic young people themselves. Naomi puts this perfectly when she says:

> *It's not that I don't like having communication cards or a whiteboard or anything else people think might help. It's actually that it's me expected to change and do all the work. It's me expected to overcome anxiety and step up.*

It's me pressured to do better all the time. It's me that's expected to change when it's them who need to change not me!

There's no point in expensive iPad apps or fancy laminated cards or anything else people think might help ME. What would actually help is feeling accepted, feeling that people genuinely care about me, know me and an atmosphere of calm and support. If that was in place in every class with every teacher then I would feel comfortable communicating in any way I could. I would nod, smile, write or type things or whatever.

The more things they give me the more pressure I feel and the bigger the demand. Talk to me, like me, and accept me. If people change to do that then they might see a very different me altogether.

*(Naomi, aged 12) www.facebook.com
/305729562884030/posts/3748956358561316/?d=n*

7

ORGANISATION AND ROUTINES

A classroom runs on routines. Teachers rely on children learning these routines and what is expected of them and then carrying those expectations out each time the relevant instructions are given. As children grow through the primary years, we start to expect that they will take some initiative to do these routines, like lining up or tidying up. Teaching staff can become quite perturbed and cross with children who fail to follow the cues, do the expected routines or seem disorganised. Because, surely, "by this age they should be able to do that?" The difficulty for autistic children is conforming to the expectations based on neurotypical norms and development.

EXECUTIVE FUNCTIONS AND AUTISM

Executive functions are the brain functions we use to predict, plan, work out how long something will take, monitor how well we are doing, use our working memory and past experiences to apply to something new and motivate ourselves to start and eventually finish something. Executive functions help us monitor our attention and focus and are skills that are developing throughout childhood into adulthood. Our approach to learning assumes children have typically developing executive functions. I often hear people say, "they should be able to do this or that at this age".

Some autistic children develop these executive function skills more slowly and unevenly than those with neurotypical development, and others will have these challenges for their whole lives. To blame a child for not being able to do something they are not developmentally able to do is wrong. These executive function challenges are very common in pupils with

DOI: 10.4324/9781003280064-10

attention deficit hyperactivity disorder (ADHD) too, and many autistic children have a dual diagnosis of autism and ADHD.

This affects our daily class management and organisation of teaching and learning. Structure and meaning are important to autistic children. Familiarity and predictability are anchor points for them to manage in a largely unpredictable world. To support autistic children who struggle to plan and be organised we can provide scaffolding.

> "Scaffolding" is a metaphor for temporary support that is removed when it is no longer required. Initially, a teacher would provide enough support so that pupils can successfully complete tasks that they could not do independently. This requires effective assessment to gain a precise understanding of the pupil's current capabilities.
>
> *(EEF, 2022)*

Examples can be:

- A written list to follow, or a visual sequence of pictures (give one instruction at a time, draw coloured boxes around parts of a worksheet and ask them to do one box at a time).
- Writing frames, partially completed examples, vocabulary prompts, sentence starters, writing about things they know a lot about to get the structure of the writing established.
- Reminders of what equipment is needed presented in pictures, symbols or lists that are taped to their books.
- Scaffolding listening and class discussion through giving the child a whiteboard to write key points on, or giving them an object that relates to the topic to hold or even a key word to listen out for as you speak.
- Specifically teaching the routines and rules that you want your children to follow as they start the year with you is the easiest way to check that all the children understand your expectations. Autistic children may need additional support through a visual schedule to remind them and let them 'see' the steps of the routine.

- If a child is struggling with organisation and routines we can work with parents and ask questions together such as:
    - Are there any sensory challenges for them?
    - Do they understand why they are being asked to do the thing you are asking?
    - Have you rushed them?
    - Are they struggling with the other children being too close to them?
    - Are the other children doing something that makes them feel unsafe?
    - Are they so interested in something else that they can't switch attention to something you want them to?
    - Are they distracted by their own thoughts or the sensory triggers in the classroom?
    - Are they anxious and worried?

In the early years you can teach sequences of actions that make a routine by using visuals. First, check that the sensory and environmental conditions are good for the child, make sure they are in a calm and receptive condition, and then show them the steps of the task in your visual sequence. At first it is best to do all the steps together – ticking off or taking off a Velcro strip for each symbol as you do it. As the child gets used to the sequence you can add in that they do the last step themselves. This means that they do the most successful step, the one that completes the task. Then you can enable them to do the last two, and then the last three steps. If you have no more than four or five steps, the routine or task can be learned and remembered. It is best to start something simple in two steps if you are not sure how much the child will be able to manage. This is often called 'backwards-chaining.'

Routines in the school day are predictable anchor points for autistic children, but can also be chaotic and overwhelming. The tidy up time when children seem to whizz around the classroom, or the home time when all the chairs are scraping and the noise is like a thunderstorm, can cause such sensory anxiety for autistic children. Putting some thought into how you can make

Figure 7.1 Example of a sequence that can be taught using backwards chaining.

these times quiet, calm and structured will be helpful for the whole class. Some examples are:

- Give each child or group of children a specific task at tidying up time. Make it very specific, such as putting all the bricks on the floor into the red box. Make it clear that when they have done their task, they have finished. Let them know what they should do next.
- Walking down the corridors can be done as a game with certain movements or chants, or as a march to help the children keep the space between them and have a purposeful activity to do as they move between places.
- Let the autistic child be first (or last) in the line, or the door monitor. Let them go before everyone else, or find another way to give them some order and control so that they can cope with the unpredictability. To develop flexibility the child may need rules to structure that, such as "you can choose to be first, second or third in the line," or a number in the line for each day of the week. Design a plan with your pupil.
- In an older class, each table of children could have a 'finished' box in the middle of the table so that they all put their

work in a specific place. Alternatively, use magazine holders for different subject books.

- Have all the usual equipment the group needs in a central box on each table which can work well, but also can clutter the table and make it difficult for everyone to have their own space. If you have room, consider putting a small cupboard or bookshelf by each table so that they can put their finished box, their equipment and visuals they are not using in or on there, leaving their workspace clutter-free and sensorily calm.

COMMUNICATION

So many professionals talk about a visual timetable, but I want to explain how to use them properly. In any age group, **the benefit of a visual timetable is only realised when you refer to it at EVERY transition point** and when children are taught to check it for information.

- **Taking the activity picture off the timetable (usually posted into a 'finished pocket') enables children to easily see where in the day they are up to because the first picture they see is what is currently happening. This reduces the cognitive load of having to scan the timetable to see where they are up to and enables a faster response**.
- A visual timetable works best when it is in front of the child as they are not then having to locate and track it on a visually distracting wall. You can theme it to their interests, and it doesn't really matter if it is vertical or horizontal as long as it is easy for them to track (top to bottom as a list or left to right as in reading something).
- Add the child's sensory breaks and other important activities for them, including a 'home' symbol, so they can be sure when those are going to happen.
- Visual timetables can **scaffold executive function skills**. Encourage the child to manage the timetable themselves by ticking off or taking off what they have finished or completed. This will enable them to manage transitions and know when changes may be happening. A change to any familiar schedule may need a clear visual reminder to help them understand what is happening and how to cope.

DOI: 10.4324/9781003280064-11

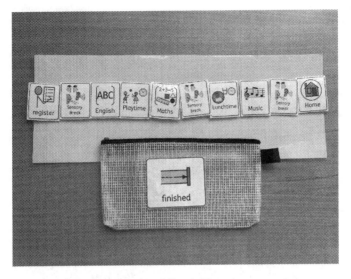

Figure 8.1 Example of a visual timetable.

- Some autistic children are very good at committing the schedule to memory, **but be careful not to assume that they don't need a visual timetable to refer to**. Ask them what helps.
- In the year before high school, we would recommend using a full-week visual timetable so that the child is familiar with looking at a whole week in preparation for going to high school. A 'to do' list alongside this can help a child organise a project or task into more manageable chunks and self-monitor where they are up to and what to do next.

> *I love my timetable; I can see when my sensory breaks are coming and that helps me cope with the rubbish lessons a bit better.*
>
> *(Autistic child, aged six)*

Visual timetables do need to be used with a caveat. If you forget to change the schedule for that day, if you put something on the timetable and it doesn't happen, or if a change happens and you forget to prepare the child for that – it may only cause more stress and anxiety for the child. As with all practical supports, we must make sure that it is meaningful and useful for the autistic child. Always monitor and ask the child what works for them and how it makes things easier or whether a support just increases their anxiety and stress. Please don't keep doing something just because a visiting professional told you to do so. Give it a try, be consistent and always involve the child in evaluating whether it is successful or not.

OTHER WAYS TO SUPPORT COMMUNICATION

As a teacher or teaching assistant, our main tool is language – we talk to explain, to give instructions, to build relationships, to manage good order in the classroom and to give feedback to our pupils. It can help to take the burden of using verbal language off pupils and explain the different ways they can communicate with us and each other. This could be through writing notes to each other, sorting pictures or symbols into categories, drawing pictures or just playing alongside each other with something like Lego or sensory toys. When they don't understand it can be difficult for them to ask for help, and we need to be the ones who are sensitive to how they communicate through their behaviour or non-verbal communication so that we can step in to help before the child gets to the point that it is unmanageable for them. They may have phrases and repetitive vocalisations that communicate anything from "I am struggling," to "I am enjoying this," and knowing the difference is useful to any adult working with them.

CLASSROOM VISUALS

In the early years, use visuals purposely to encourage verbal or other communication. Visual Talk Mats for each activity area can provide children with clear vocabulary to help them talk about the activity. For example, a brick building area can have pictures with words for shapes, sizes and positions with symbols for the children to understand the words. The staff would be able to model these by pointing out the words whilst they play with the children. You can also have some basic 'choice' and 'asking' words on display, such as "can I play?" "my turn next," "wait" and "yes" or "no."

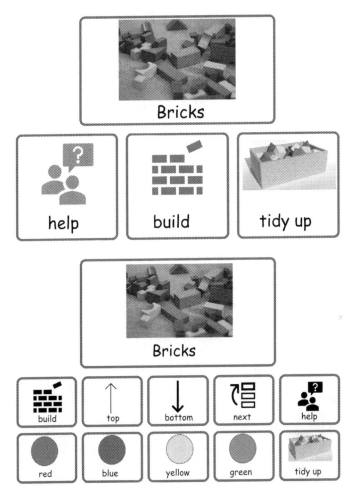

Figure 8.2 Examples of vocabulary mats that can accompany an activity table.

In all years, the speech and language approaches that are for neurotypical children could be less than helpful to autistic children (Lees, nd). The type of support needed may depend on whether the professionals think the child may be autistic, even if they are undiagnosed. A speech and language therapist (SLT) may introduce you to visuals or software on an iPad which needs a consistent and integrated effort from all staff in the setting, at all times. It is no use giving a child access to communication that is only available to them for part of the day. When we teach them a way of communicating, it has to be responded to and be effective for the child. It has to build up from their natural way of communicating, which we need to have tuned into first. We need to listen to their "no." When a child refuses or resists we need to ask some important questions. Start with a simple, "Why?" and "What is difficult for the child?"

USEFUL VERBAL COMMUNICATION

In order to engage the child in our learning activities, guiding them into opportunities and tasks needs a careful approach. Making it very clear what you are doing, what it is helping them learn and how long or how much there is to do right from the start. The language of 'first and then' can be very helpful, taking care to break down the tasks and not overload the child with future demands. When I was a mainstream class teacher I found the following tips very useful for all children in my class:

- Say exactly what you want and show them how to do it.
- Say exactly what you mean and keep sentences short when giving instructions. I often find myself saying "and that means ... "
- Leave them time to process and don't jump in too quickly with reminders. Don't assume they didn't hear you.
- When a child has understood your instruction and is doing what you asked, don't interrupt them with more language to process. Being chatty during an activity isn't helpful for children struggling to understand.

- For those who do copy language, instead of asking them lots of questions, comment on what you notice, e.g., "the doll is on the bed." Or "the tower is getting taller." This way you are modelling language for them to understand in context.
- Be careful not to frame instructions as questions. Saying "do you want to put your coat on?" when you mean "you have to put your coat on" is confusing. If the child is comfortable wearing a coat (do check), then it is much better to say, "it's time to put your coat on, do you need help?"
- Be aware of literal understanding. If you say "do you want me to put your coat on?" an autistic child may well be expecting you to wear their coat!
- A non-verbal child is not a non-understanding child. Be careful what you say about the child and remember they may have super-sensitive hearing. They will know when you are talking about them, so be sure to say good and affirmative things about them.

> Thinking back, clearer instructions would have made primary school easier. Sometimes when I do not fully understand the work, I will simply not do any of it.
>> (Jackson, aged 21, reflecting on his primary school experience)

TEACHING THE CURRICULUM

There are many theories about how autistic children learn, and there is evidence to support and discredit all of them. We have seen good support and happy learners when some strategies are in place, such as a visual vocabulary mat or a TEACCH (originally this stood for 'Treatment and Education of Autistic and related Communications Handicapped Children') (Mesibov, 2015) work system, but then the same strategies and support won't be effective for another autistic child. In my experience, there are some general principles we can follow in setting up a classroom for an autistic child as long as we keep asking, "How is this support strategy helping the child?"

Wellbeing is the first foundation of being able to learn. Getting the environment, organisation and sensory regulation times right for your autistic child will give them a better space to be able to learn. Have you ever been so stressed that you can't focus or function at your job or even daily living demands? That is the most common experience of autistic children in schools. It's why when we build support programmes for autistic children they need to first feel safe in order to be able to learn.

MOTIVATION

The key to motivation for many autistic children is to make meaningful links to their concrete experience and knowledge. Where their imagination goes, go there with them. In my experience, primary teachers are an imaginative lot, and I have seen some stunning examples of engaging autistic children in learning through their interests.

DOI: 10.4324/9781003280064-12

One of my schools did this with an autistic pupil who loved the London Underground. Once his teachers understood that this could engage him, they themed the class timetable on a London line with stations as the next stopping point of the daily schedule. They managed to link every single topic to the Underground or to London which helped this child go from barely engaging in any class learning to being fully involved in every lesson. As a result, the whole class learned a lot about London and their topic on the Great Fire was a huge success. The pupil cannot wait until the last year of primary school when they will go on the London trip. The other children are already asking him to be their guide.

When there are no obvious links and the child cannot see the purpose of a topic or subject, it will be important to support them through that subject. For subjects such as maths or writing, we may need further assessments in case they have undiagnosed dyslexia or dyscalculia. For subjects such as PE there could be many sensory and physical reasons why it is difficult for them. Autistic children are so different (not all are maths geniuses), and will have preferences and things they are not interested in like any other child. Some do have areas of exceptional ability, but many will be of average ability or have learning disabilities. Being flexible is the key. **Don't be afraid of changing things so that the child can learn in the way they learn, even if that looks different from the rest of the class**. This doesn't mean that autistic children won't join in with what the rest of the class is doing. If you get it right for them, they may love to do what you have planned for the whole class. Some will feel terrified of being different and work very hard to fit in. That's **masking**, and then the motivation for learning becomes managing anxiety, rather than the love of learning. Even if our adjustments are subtle, however you do it, try to make their interests and wellbeing fit in with what you are teaching. They will benefit from that forever.

> There was no one thing that she did that made me trust her. It was all of the little things she did over the course of the year. For example, I used to have to sit at the front of the class right beside the teacher's desk. In her class, I was allowed to sit along the wall of the classroom in the very back but it was not quite in the corner of the room. I was able to see everyone without them seeing me.
>
> She never embarrassed me by making me get up and answer questions. She allowed me to read books or colour whenever I was bored. I was allowed the freedom to be myself which made me more willing to tolerate what was going on around me.
>
> *(Claire Sainsbury, 2009)*

In these primary years children are required to demonstrate that they have learned neurotypical social conventions such as greetings, manners, turn taking, waiting, paying attention. However, one of the ways we assess attention is through children looking at the teacher. This can be hugely problematic for autistic children because eye contact can be extremely uncomfortable. Many autistic children cannot pay attention if the demand is to give eye contact, because this is so painful for them. And in truth, why do you have to look to be able to listen and understand? Please don't ever demand eye contact from autistic children; instead, understand how they learn and what helps them concentrate and listen.

> *What do you want teachers to know?*
>
> That I am built different and my brain does not work the same as neurotypical people and I may need additional support and extra care. For them to know EYE CONTACT IS NOT IMPORTANT!!!!
>
> *(Autistic child, Spectrum Gaming)*

THE EARLY YEARS CURRICULUM

Play is at the heart of learning in the early years, but increasingly I see children being asked to sit and do directed tasks for longer to meet the demands of an imposed curriculum and targets. In the UK, daily phonic teaching is mandatory and takes up a good chunk of time each day, whilst pre-reading and writing activities are a major focus. Whilst autistic children do learn through play, their play may look different to that of their neurotypical peers. We should be allowing them to learn the way they play, to investigate and to explore through their senses in this rich environment that we create for them. Sadly, there is a lot of effort made to try and make autistic children play in what is perceived to be a neurotypical way, and our assessments and recording of what they achieve only lead to the child being seen as not meeting the expected standards or development levels. This is a huge problem throughout most education systems.

Generally, an autistic child "processes the world in smaller, detailed moments before conceptualising the whole. Processing and understanding the components that make up the whole are generally processed through sensory self-exploration rather than a shared experience" (Conn, 2015).

Their experience of learning is often solitary or alongside others, but it is no less valuable. Autistic children need to conceptualise the world in a way they can understand before making attempts to interact with others. Some are observers and imitators of other children. These are the children who seem to be doing 'fine' and mostly managing to get by, and they are often quick learners of the curriculum content. Other autistic children obviously struggle to understand the neurotypical social world and their attempts to interact with others are seen as clumsy or aggressive.

Play the way they play. Imitate, interact and play alongside the autistic child (or the child who seems different and has not yet been diagnosed) and create a bubble of shared attention. The child should lead and you should follow. It can be very difficult to do this if you are only intent on getting children to come to the learning/phonics/maths table to do a prescriptive activity. You are likely to meet resistance or even cause distress to a child who may be autistic. How you plan for this when all the other children are following your routines, coming to the tables without resistance and sitting on the carpet together, is a challenge, but starting with a simple 'companionship' approach can enable you to draw an autistic child in to the learning landscape that you are creating, and show them that their enthusiasms fit in there too.

> *I might hit developmental and societal milestones in a different order than my peers, but I am able to accomplish these small victories on my own time.*
>
> *(Haley Moss, livingautism.com)*

THE PRIMARY CURRICULUM

Whatever curriculum your school has in place, whether that is a national curriculum or a school-based curriculum, a curriculum is designed for all children to follow. Their progress is assessed by the curriculum rules, and we make judgements on the child's intelligence and ability based on our assessments of the curriculum targets. These curriculums are based on neurotypical child development, along with government political objectives and educational research that is in fashion at the time. I have been teaching for over 30 years and have seen educational fashions swing in different directions over that time. Generally, though, teachers want children to learn and teachers want children to love learning.

Recent theories have described how monotropic processing is a feature of many autistic persons' processing. This means that their attention may be more focussed on specific areas of interest, things they notice and are motivated by. This is used to explain why autistic people often seem to stay focussed, or perhaps appear to be 'stuck' on one thing. They may seem obsessed with a particular topic, or only able to focus on certain details, rather than seeing the bigger picture (Murray, Lesser and Lawson, 2005). For them it is a strength, an ability to learn something in depth and to gain joy from knowing and doing something that they are passionate about. Being monotropic can impact on their language processing, especially when language is coming from multiple sources or social interactions and impacts on their ability to switch attention to something else. There are many demands on them to do these things in school. When teachers interrupt a child working on a task, it can disrupt their ability to refocus on the task. Some autistic children have to finish a task before moving on to something else and can become very distressed if we insist that they will be able to finish it later. Neurotypical children can usually work in a polytropic way, being able to give attention to multiple items and ideas at the same time. We tend to teach to this approach and expect that children can make the links, switch attention and work with multiple ideas and topics to generalise their learning.

If we work with the autistic child's interests, and the way they can focus that attention in a monotropic way, we are more likely to enable them to learn and thrive in their learning. Their specialist interests, passions for "enthusiasms" as Prizant (2022) calls them, are a gift to us as teachers if we know how to harness them. Rather than seeming to have to always be redirecting the child because they want to talk about their interests, use that as a key connection point with them, bring it into discussions and make links in the learning topic and it will be a good way of keeping their interest in topics they might find hard to connect with. Most curriculums can be flexible and adapted to make them accessible to autistic learners. We may have to teach a topic but there is usually freedom to teach it in creative ways.

As a creative teacher, you have permission to explore other ways of recording in the wider curriculum.

- Using technology, from PowerPoints to film making, can be a great way for some autistic children to demonstrate what they have learned (and maybe teach you something along the way).
- Recording what they want to say, drawing it, making things and, most importantly, giving them time to process what you are teaching them can make a difference in any subject or topic.
- Some autistic pupils are bored in your lessons and long to be challenged, so prepare problems to solve and challenges that they can research for themselves, particularly when they can relate the task to their own interests.

- Use mapping to show how topics within a subject are linked, and explain when things are concrete or abstract such as in maths.

Stepping outside the box you as a teacher have been put in (to teach certain things a certain way) can be as liberating for you as it is for your pupils.

> I was the only intelligent one there and I was always refused when I wanted to do work that challenged me ... so the lack of, "hey, I guess you can add numbers, so here's something extra hard and challenging for you to explore."
> (Autistic child, Spectrum Gaming)

WRITING

Writing underpins so much of our curriculum and learning expectations that I wanted to add a chapter just on this. It is a myth that autistic people have mathematical or scientific minds rather than an aptitude for the creative arts or writing skills. Autistic children will all be different; some have wonderful and imaginative writing, can focus well on a topic and love to be able to write from their imagination. Autistic children can excel in story writing and poetry. I keep in touch with an ex-student who is studying creative writing at university. Other autistic children struggle with writing: the coming up with ideas, understanding the point, composition, organisation of a piece of writing and, of course, handwriting. There are so many demands to include correct spellings, punctuation and grammar as well as the content needing to be 'creative.' Questions about supporting writing are the most common areas of learning support my team are asked about, and the main areas of difference and difficulty I have noticed are as follows.

1. Handwriting

Some autistic children have hypermobile joints which make writing difficult and painful. This may be diagnosed as Ehlers-Danlos syndromes. They may have undiagnosed dyspraxia. Some autistic children struggle with other sensory elements such as the texture of a pencil, the pressure needed on it and the spatial awareness of letters on the paper. Others may have a different way of holding a pencil and cannot manage the tripod grip that we might be trying to get them to use. To help them we would first check the

DOI: 10.4324/9781003280064-13

equipment – is it the paper or the writing tool that is the problem? Or is it the holding of the pencil and the motor movement that is the problem? Sometimes it could just be that the child cannot remember what the letters look like. Some autistic children have beautiful, clear handwriting and love writing over having to speak.

- Some children have been helped by being able to do their writing on a whiteboard or on different coloured or textured paper with a felt-tip or roller ball pen instead of a pencil. Let them use their preferred writing tool. Please get rid of pen-licences in your school – they are discriminatory against children with sensory-motor difficulties.

- The child may need support to develop their balance, gross motor coordination, tracking and core strength through a sensory diet. An occupational therapist would advise on this. Being able to have the core strength and balance to sit correctly is part of the handwriting posture development.

- We might support with more sensory and fine motor activities. Some may benefit from these to strengthen their hand muscles and awareness of what their hand is doing when writing. These are often supported by an occupational therapist, but you can also use programmes such as www.spreadthehappiness.co.uk/dough-disco/.

- We might give the child a visual alphabet strip so that they can see the letters and have a visual reminder to enable them to get on with the writing.

- We would also encourage the teacher to introduce technology. We have to weigh up whether the effort we are putting into writing with a pen or pencil is worth the output. It just could be better to free up the child to write by giving them access to a laptop, speech-to-text facility or a symbol-supported software such as Widgit or Clicker, whilst still working on their motor stability and skills.

I hate writing. The day my teacher let me use a laptop was like heaven. I had already taught myself to type and I love the spell checker. My mum said it might stop me being able to spell in tests, but my teacher said I can use it in some tests as it is the usual way I work.

(Autistic child, aged eight)

2. Organisation of writing

Those autistic children who have executive function diffi-culties are likely to find the process of doing writing tasks difficult, despite having lots of ideas for the story. Knowing where to start, how to break the content into a structure that will flow, how to read it back and check for that flow or any mistakes, and when to finish are all elements we may need to scaffold. There is the added pressure of trying to work out the unspoken expectations of the teacher – what the teacher thinks is 'correct' may be not understood by the autistic child. How do you create a story whilst check-ing your spelling and punctuation? The working memory to keep track of where they were up to in the story (especially if their attention is interrupted) can easily be lost. Some autistic children develop a fear of having to correct their work to the extent that they may refuse to go back to it when it is finished, or sometimes that fear can prevent them from even starting.

- Scaffold executive functions by breaking the writing task into clear steps. Even using first, next, last or a beginning, middle and end can be helpful.
- Use writing frames which set out the structure for the child. If you use one writing frame consistently, the child can get used to that and hopefully will be able to structure a piece of writing using that structure more independently and from memory as they get older.
- Some children need to go back to the very beginning of writing to reinforce their understanding of sentence structure and the reasons for punctuation. With the uneven development many autistic children have, they

may have missed out on some key learning earlier in their education. We have found using **colourful semantics** useful for this. Colourful semantics are a system where the child makes up sentences with a colour for each element of the sentence, such as who, what and when. This can develop into using colours for starters, verbs, adjectives and other grammatical elements. These also help those gestalt language learners break down the whole sentence into the different words. It is worth discussing this with a speech and language therapist if you think this could help your autistic child.

3. Inference, fiction and facts

We have discussed a lot about using an autistic child's interests and enthusiasms to engage them in learning. Sometimes autistic children can struggle with fiction because to them it isn't true and is therefore difficult to work with. Other autistic children are able to make up amazing stories and fantasies but may struggle to follow a prescribed theme or idea for a story. I once read an amazing piece of writing from an autistic child which we later realised was the story of the latest Spiderman film. He had just changed the character's name and used what he knew from the film for his ideas of what happened in the story. I know many authors and they say that there are only so many story scripts out there. For some autistic children giving them permission to borrow ideas from films and stories that they love can be a great way to develop their writing. Some autistic children can only deal with what is in their own experience and therefore that is where we would start from.

Another difficulty that some autistic children have in composing writing is needing to tell you all the details. Being able to summarise or suggest an idea involves being able to understand what the reader might need to be able to get an idea of what you're talking about. Many autistic children will want to make sure that the reader knows as much as they do on the topic. If this is a difficulty in class because of time then it may be useful to ask the child to focus on one aspect of the topic. Most targets or learning objectives that we are working on in a lesson can be adapted to many different subjects, so don't be afraid of being flexible in what the child actually writes about. Understanding the meaning of words can be very difficult for some autistic children who would much prefer things to say what they mean.

- To build up their experience on vocabulary use visuals, videos and practical experiences to give them an idea of what the experience involves and is like so they can write about it. An example would be having to write about a circus when the child has never been to a circus, so watching a video to support that and give them the vocabulary and knowledge that they would need.
- Idioms and metaphors can also be difficult, so teach the class what they mean. Play with language, explaining meaning as you go along.

Tomas moved into the junior class in a small school, unable to write anything without constant prompting from his teaching assistant. Any writing was laborious, exhausting and unfulfilling. Tomas was a bright child and very gifted in music and languages. We realised that Tomas was struggling with the formation of sentences and coping with the imaginative construction of a piece of writing. We broke these concepts down, and put in place an activity that he did every day. He brought a photograph from home, therefore writing about something that he was very familiar with. He and his teaching assistant discussed the photo and wrote key vocabulary words around it so that he could use those in his writing. The next step was to use a writing frame that always had the same structure and three words; "first, next, last" with a clear space to write by each. His teaching assistant also did some work with him on sentence starters, and had a colour-coded visual reminder of what verbs and adjectives were. With this structure, Tomas was soon writing three full sentences that flowed and linked together based on his photograph. This preparation enabled Tomas to write much longer pieces of coherent writing by the time he left the school four years later.

11

MATHS AND TESTS

It is a myth that all autistic people are great mathematicians or scientists. And yet, some are! Autistic children may have an affinity for numbers and mathematics; they may be able to see how the numbers work together and be able to do complex calculations in their head. In the early years I have worked with autistic children who know all the numbers to 1,000 and beyond and spend a lot of time counting, writing and playing with numbers. I have known nine- and ten-year-old autistic children capable of doing some A-level maths. However, there are just as many autistic children who struggle to grasp mathematical concepts and may have difficulty throughout their education with this subject.

Maths is a logical subject but it also has many abstract concepts and calculations that do not relate to actual physical contexts. It is this switch from the concrete to the abstract that can cause many children difficulties. With autistic children there are some key strategies that can support their grasp and understanding.

- If they love numbers and have a greater ability than the class, support this and, whilst checking their understanding, accept that some things are natural to them and explaining it to someone else is a different skill altogether. Plan to extend and develop their skills before they become bored and frustrated in regular lessons.
- Relate the numbers to something concrete and interesting to them right from the beginning. Seeing the point of the calculation or concept in the real world can help all children.

DOI: 10.4324/9781003280064-14

- Many schemes now use concrete apparatus which can help children form a visual concept of things like number bonds and place value. Make these available in every lesson and model how to use them as you explain the maths lesson.
- Break the lesson into smaller chunks. Rather than sitting for a long explanation, explain one thing, then get the children to practise. Start with going over what you have learned before (retrieval) that links to this lesson. Then move on to the next part in the same way.
- Introducing new concepts and processes may need additional practice for autistic children. The pace of lessons can be so fast that we need to build this time to process a new idea or way of working for autistic children.
- Make connections clear. Show a visual map of how the work they have done before links to what they are doing now; for example, how the underpinning of sharing out pizza relates to fractions and percentages. This can help identify any gaps in knowledge that the child may have.
- Explain phrases and words as you go along, particularly when there is a word that means something different in maths than in other contexts. For example, 'sum' and 'some,' or 'table' and 'table.'
- Give autistic children a word list of key mathematical vocabulary. Preferably with a symbol or example of what it means. We put these on a keyring so they can refer to it at every lesson.
- To support problem-solving, especially word problems, give the child two highlighters. Use one colour to highlight the numbers in the problem, and the other to highlight the operations, or what they need to do with the numbers. For many autistic children, the extra words around a problem are distracting and confusing.
- Autistic children are often unable to say that they don't understand something and will often try to apply the things they do understand to an unfamiliar problem. Understanding this can help us teach them by asking them first, "what do you know?" Or "what did you do with these numbers?"

There is a fallacy that autistic children cannot learn or understand abstract concepts. This is incorrect. What autistic children often struggle to understand is not the abstract concept itself, but rather when they are not taught that something is an abstract concept. In this case, autistic children can think that they are expected to understand abstract concepts in the same way as concrete ideas ... **Students will always resort to the most familiar thing that they are sure of, even when that is not what the question requires**. Even when a child understands in a passive way when the teacher explains a concept, it does not mean they will remember it and be able to apply it later on.

(Forbes, 2022)

TESTS

Autistic children can find tests very stressful. One of the main reasons for this is usually that tests are something different and there is a time pressure. Autistic children easily pick up that there is an expectation and that it is important. Often, as teachers, we keep telling children how important these tests are. Autistic children (and I would argue most children) don't really understand what tests are FOR. Fear of failure can be a factor, as well as finding it difficult to switch attention from question to question, in the timeframe. Add to that any sensory challenges and difficulties with writing as explained in the previous chapter, and it isn't hard to see why assessments and tests are difficult for autistic children. None of us do well when we are stressed.

However, there is the additional factor of tests being designed for measuring a neurotypical standard. **The problem is not that our autistic children are below the standard, but that the standard has not been designed to include autistic children**.

TIME PRESSURE

The timing and shifting attention from question to question is a lot of pressure and the autistic brain may not work naturally in this mode. When we are stressed, there is less logical thinking and, conversely, autistic children may be too logical and answer a question literally when it actually means something else. I really have seen papers where an autistic child has answered a question such as "can you explain … " with a simple "yes." Tests are usually not the best way for an autistic child to show you what they have learned. There will be some autistic children who can do tests well, and may even enjoy the peace and quiet of a test lesson, but many more will not.

> Many autistic learners are verbal processors. For example, sitting maths tests in silence means that they are automatically at a huge disadvantage. This is something I have become increasingly aware of over my years of teaching, and this is not something that students grow out of.
>
> *(Forbes, 2022)*

WAYS TO SUPPORT ASSESSMENTS AND TESTING

- Give the autistic child plenty of notice and a visual explanation of what the assessment will be like, how long it will take and what it is helping the assessor learn about them.
- In all assessments, consider breaking the assessment into smaller chunks with sensory breaks in between.
- When a visiting professional is coming, ask them to send a photo and outline of what they are going to do to show the child beforehand (I have been doing this with great effect when the child gets to read it before I arrive).
- Consider adapting the assessment to relate it to the interests of the child if you can. An autistic child knew all the letter sounds and phonic blends in class and could read well, but could not do the test where he had to 'perform' these out of context.
- Find out what accommodations you can make for national tests and apply for them early. Give the child a better chance by making it like their usual way of working. If they

use a laptop, then let them do tests on a laptop. These are all legal reasonable adjustments and can help a child manage a test or exam.

- Find alternative ways to show what the child knows and report this to parents. They may find seeing their child's report full of 'does not meet expectations' very worrying.
- Autistic children may need longer time and to be taught what the language of a test means they need to do (e.g., "can you explain?" means you have to write an explanation).

Chris Bonello, an autistic teacher, says we should keep tests in perspective: they only measure certain things, not how brilliant we are at many other things. I love to give out his letter to Year 6 children every year: https://autisticnotweird.com/sats/.

12

SUPPORTING BEHAVIOUR

Whenever I am asked to help an autistic child whose behaviour is 'challenging' or 'concerning' for the school and for parents, we always first work through the autism needs of the child (communication, sensory, social, emotional, learning) and make sure that they are being met appropriately. We check they are not in pain or being bullied and that they are not being punished for being unable to cope with school.

All I have written about in this book IS our behaviour support. When we are proactive and get things as right as we can for the child, in many cases, the behaviours that were concerning us, were actually the child's communication. They were not coping with school, and we are the ones who can do all we can to change that.

BEING A BEHAVIOUR DETECTIVE

We should be looking at behaviour as if the child is communicating to us, or that they are not coping well with something. They are therefore not a 'problem' to be fixed, or someone doing something 'wrong,' but the behaviour is a sign that something isn't working.

When looking at behaviour, understanding the context is vital. This means knowing about the individual and their needs, but equally considering the environment. Asking pertinent questions can help us work out what help our autistic child will need and respond best to. Being PROACTIVE means being CURIOUS and REFLECTIVE:

- How much stress is 'in the bucket' already?
- Why did they do that?

DOI: 10.4324/9781003280064-15

- What are they trying to communicate?
- What do I already know about this child and how they react in different situations? Have we put them in a situation they cannot tolerate right now?
- Are **my** tolerance/arousal levels at the right stage to support the child through this?
- Should I back off/give processing time/communicate in a different way (e.g., write a note)?
- Have we got a way out plan?
- What have we done before that worked?
- What am I assuming without realising?

If others are getting hurt or the child is self-harming, then making sure they are safe is the first concern. We often strip back the demands we can see are obviously causing distress, and then work to reintroduce them as we work out what will make them work better. We may take some demands away permanently, such as expectations to sit with the class on the carpet, go to assembly or do homework.

For autistic children, consequences or punishments are external reactions to something that was for them a very logical action. School systems tend to have negative consequences for work not completed or behaviours that break the rules. Even with the best will in the world, they are not always clear or applied consistently. Autistic children are often confused by and even terrified of reactions to something that has caused them distress, such as someone getting in their way or not understanding a piece of work. I get asked by a lot of teaching staff, "how can we make them understand the consequences of their actions?" This is a much more complex question than just teaching an autistic child that what they do has an impact on others. It is usually used to ask why we are not punishing a child for their wrongdoing. **We can be meeting NEED with discipline, and wonder why it doesn't make the child behave better**. Discipline often keeps the child in a state of high anxiety, feeling unsafe and unable to regulate.

The reasons why an autistic child does something, the behaviour that we see, has an autistic reason behind it. Consider the following example.

I was called into a school that needed help to manage an autistic child's behaviour. The child was trying to control her teaching assistant, regularly hitting her and headbutting her if she didn't get her own way. She was on the verge of being excluded but the school wanted to work through this with her parents and myself.

We realised that we could be sure the child was unable to think her actions through at the moment she was hitting out, and that she felt a great lot of shame when she got home. Therefore, we reassessed the child's communication, sensory needs and organisation skills.

We discovered that the move to Year 5 had been traumatic for the girl. She had been given a new teaching assistant while her regular and most trusted TA had been off for an operation. This had not been a successful relationship and the girl had become very withdrawn. When the old TA came back, the child was so anxious that the TA would go off again and so worried that another person would look after her. However, she could not find the way to communicate that and instead took out her anxiety on the person she felt safe with and trusted the most – her beloved TA.

Now we knew what had happened, we could work with the child, her parents and the TA to move forward, develop trusting relationships with other staff in the school and give the child easier ways of communicating her worries.

- Understand how your autistic child relates to the rules. Some will want to keep them consistently and become upset when others do not. They may become very frustrated and angry with this.
- Work with parents to collate all the information you can. If the child is fine at home and not at school it is often the school environment and the demands of the school day that can be causing the difficulties. Similarly, if the child is fine at school but not at home, the same reasons could apply.

- We may need to teach the child specifically how to manage the rules and routines of the classroom whilst making reasonable adjustments to the consequences of general rules to allow for their needs.
- Make a safe place for the child that they can go to when things are too much for them. Lower demands and reassure them. This can be an effective response for a child who runs out of class or out of school. A safe person they can talk to can make all the difference too.

Behaviour management techniques that are clear and well explained can support autistic children when school is generally working well for them. However, the majority of autistic children whose behaviour has been 'concerning' and 'challenging' that I have known in all these years, have been distressed, overwhelmed and anxious within an environment and system that is creating an intolerable daily experience for them. This is not to blame any teacher or school, but to highlight that it is not the child or parents that are to blame. Working together to meet the child's needs (or in some situations, to find a more specialist school) is the way forward. In a busy classroom where teachers cannot see everything or know everything that is going on with all the children, teamwork between home and school, as well as the Special Educational Needs Co-ordinator (SENCO) and outside professionals, is vital. It also has to centre on understanding the child and their perspective first.

> The visual traffic light system did not always encourage good behaviour for me, as I recall receiving detention a few times. For detention, you were sent to either a small room, the head teacher's office. Although I used to fear the word, it was sometimes a relief to be removed from the room or playground: it became a quiet place where I could go to get away from what was causing my stress and anxiety.
>
> (Jackson aged 21, recalling his primary
> school experience)

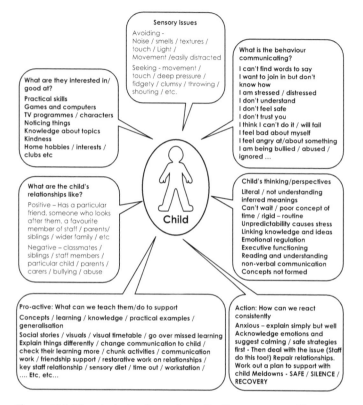

Sensory issues
Avoiding -
Noise / smells / textures /
touch / Light /
Movement /easily distracted

Seeking - movement /
touch / deep pressure /
fidgety / clumsy / throwing /
shouting / etc.

What is the behaviour communicating?
I can't find words to say
I want to join in but don't
know how
I am stressed / distressed
I don't understand
I don't feel safe
I don't trust you
I think I can't do it / will fail
I feel bad about myself
I feel angry at/about something
I am being bullied / abused /
ignored ...

What are they interested in/ good at?
Practical skills
Games and computers
TV programmes / characters
Noticing things
Knowledge about topics
Kindness
Home hobbies / interests /
clubs etc

What are the child's relationships like?
Positive – Has a particular
friend, someone who looks
after them, a favourite
member of staff / parents/
siblings / wider family / etc

Negative – classmates /
siblings / staff members /
particular child / parents /
carers / bullying / abuse

Child

Child's thinking/perspectives
Literal / not understanding
inferred meanings
Can't wait / poor concept of
time / rigid – routine
Unpredictability causes stress
Linking knowledge and ideas
Emotional regulation
Executive functioning
Reading and understanding
non-verbal communication
Concepts not formed

Pro-active: What can we teach them/do to support
Concepts / learning / knowledge / practical examples /
generalisation
Social stories / visuals / visual timetable / go over missed learning
Explain things differently / change communication to child /
check their learning more / chunk activities / communication
work / friendship support / restorative work on relationships /
key staff relationship / sensory diet / time out / workstation /
.... Etc, etc...

Action: How can we react consistently
Anxious – explain simply but well
Acknowledge emotions and
suggest calming / safe strategies
first - Then deal with the issue (Staff
do this too!) Repair relationships.
Work out a plan to support with
child Meldowns - SAFE / SILENCE /
RECOVERY

Figure 12.1 Visual behaviour investigation map with word prompts.

Figure 12.1 is a visual form that I give out when I am doing training about seeing behaviour through the autism lens, to help us be that 'detective' when the child's behaviour is concerning us. This version has some helpful comments to lead our investigations and a blank copy is available as a downloadable resource.

13

THE ROLE OF TEACHING ASSISTANTS

The presence of additional adults in a classroom of 30 or more children is varied throughout schools. Some teachers can have three or more part-time staff working in their class, others have very little additional help at all. Some children come with a 1:1 assistant and how that person interacts with the rest of the class will vary. The work done by the teaching assistant (TA) will depend on factors such as their experience, their job description, the school's policy and culture of using TAs in classes and the needs of the children in your class. I would recommend reading the research done by the Education Endowment Foundation (2018) about making the best use of TAs.

CLASS TEACHING ASSISTANTS

Teachers may want their teaching assistant to help all children who may need additional support in their class and these children may have a range of different needs. The approaches that a child with attention deficit hyperactivity disorder (ADHD) needs could be very different from a child with dyslexia, for example. Knowing all the key approaches for all the pupils in your class depends on the class teacher and teaching assistant working together. When autistic children need their sensory breaks and visual timetables managing, the teaching assistant is often the one to do this when the class teacher is teaching the whole class or working with other pupils.

- Work together as a team. Teachers, try to make sure your TA knows what you are doing in your lessons so they can read

DOI: 10.4324/9781003280064-16

through it before the lesson and start to pick out what additional support they can offer to the children who need it.

- Do some training together and share what you both learn about your autistic pupils. That may include insights from articles and books (like this one!) you read or information parents pass on to you. Please check that the things you read or are told are relevant and affirming the child. Autistic-led training is often a good way of helping you understand the experiences of your autistic pupil.
- It may be the TA is the one speaking to the parent at the end of each day and finding time to feed back to the teacher can be difficult. Try to find a way of communicating that is easy and accessible for you both. Have a policy of speaking positively over the child, especially in the child's hearing.
- Give the TA time to prepare resources within their working hours. It is unfair to expect them to do this in their own time, considering how little they are paid.
- Discuss the expectations in lessons. Many TAs think that their class teachers expect them to help the child keep up with finishing the content. This means that sometimes the TA ends up almost doing the work for the child. The process of learning is more important and giving the child the chance to work something out for themselves rather than be corrected or prompted all the time is more valuable to their learning (EEF Report, 2018).
- Encourage your TAs not to talk over you to a child whenever possible. If you are not sure what the other adult has said to the child, try to find out rather than say something that will just confuse the child further. Give TAs a whiteboard or have all staff carry a communication set of symbols that they can use when another member of staff is talking.
- Agree your approach to the child as a team. Telling an autistic child to stop stimming can be very harmful, but a TA who has not been told this may inadvertently tell the child to stop, thinking they are helping with class management.
- Communicate clearly to the autistic child what the TA is there to help them with. If the child is relying on the adults in the room, then they will feel safer when their relationship

is based on the adult sharing their interests and the child knows they are understood and supported.

- Many autistic children struggle with attention being drawn to them in front of the whole class. Teachers and TAs should have a clear plan of checking their communication and who will respond to it. You could give the child a colour-coded sign to put on their desk so they don't have to call out or put their hand up for help.

> *I had a wrist band I could turn over if I was feeling anxious. The teachers were supposed to check it and come to me when they noticed I had turned it around. This would have worked well if they had remembered to look at it.*
>
> *(Autistic child, aged 11)*

1:1 TEACHING ASSISTANTS

1:1 assistants are sometimes assigned to a child as part of their needs assessment and educational support in their EHCP or IEP. They may be part time (I know many children who have 1:1 support in the mornings during English and maths, but have no support in the afternoons) or full time. The relationship between the adult and the autistic child is absolutely the most important thing for the child. The TA needs a good understanding of the autistic spectrum but cannot rely on their knowledge of previous autistic children they have worked with. Each child will be different. This TA will often be given a lot of responsibility for differentiating the curriculum, supporting the child during routines, meeting with parents and delivering interventions that have been prescribed by other professionals such as speech and language therapists. However, the class teacher is still responsible for the educational provision of the autistic child and this relationship should be teamwork around the child. The role of a teaching assistant is a hugely demanding one.

> To do your job properly. You are going to also have to read through professional reports and understand what

they mean and what they are recommending. This could be EP reports, OT reports, physio, speech and language. You are going to have to read an educational health and care plan and understand a) your child or young person, b) what their special educational needs are, c) the desired outcomes for that child and d) what you need to do to achieve those. Some of that is going to involve delivering therapy to that child as set out by an OT, Physio or SALT. A lot of it is complex stuff.

(Mummy to Six blog, 2018)

- Set up the support plan around the child at the beginning of the year, making sure that the teamwork between the TA and the teacher is established. Agree on how the child will be supported in lessons, when interventions will take place and where, and how the autistic child's learning and pro-gress will be supported.
- Get your basics in place and make them part of your daily routine. If the child uses a visual timetable, make sure that is ready when they start in the morning. If the child is often late, then you are ready to start at the place where the class is at and can show this in the timetable. If they need certain resources, have a stack of them available for access at any time, e.g., writing frames, maths visuals, pencils, scissors, etc. Finally, make sure their sensory activities are accessi-ble, on the timetable and ready to use.
- Know your child's preferences and signs that they are starting to become overwhelmed. A good TA can usually put a regulation strategy into place (sensory break, fewer demands, going to the calm place) early enough to avoid meltdowns. This doesn't mean you will avoid all meltdowns, just that you will more often than not be able to spot early signs before the child gets to a point of no return.
- Have an agreed response if your autistic child looks like they are not coping. For example, at playtimes, arguments can often be the result of the autistic child feeling out of control, and are a product of unpredictability rather than nastiness.

- The class teacher could record (or pre-record) the lesson input on an iPad so that the autistic child and the TA can go over the lesson input again. I have seen this work really well, giving the autistic child a chance to break it down into smaller steps (tip: wear headphones to listen back to it!). Or you can send the lesson input home for parents to support the child, if that suits them.
- The TA should look to develop the problem-solving ability of the child through giving them time to think and process a task. We rush autistic children so much into getting through a task that they can become over-dependent on the adult prompting or doing something for them and so develop a kind of learned helplessness. It is better to ask key questions such as "how would you start that?" or prompt them by showing them a past piece of work to use as a template than to end up doing the work for the child.
- Autistic children should be praised for the effort and ability to think about things differently. So much of our teaching is based on an assumed outcome that we can often miss the creativity and progress that our children are making. If they produce something that looks different from what you expected, then look for the ways that it does show what they have learned.
- Don't put pressure on the autistic child by asking them lots of questions. Instead, give choices or use other communication methods such as drawing or writing. Comic strip conversations (Gray, 1994) can be helpful in exploring incidents, memories of activities or trying to work out a problem.
- Think about where you sit alongside the child. Take into consideration their toleration of eye contact, their sensory tolerances and their access to be able to interact with other children. Think about the resources you will use on a regular basis and how to store these. Sitting near a shelf or cupboard where you can have easy access to resources may be helpful. Label and make things easy to grab in the middle of a lesson. If the child has speech and language or other intervention activities, keep them in coloured folders so you can

recognise them easily. Create a visually comfortable area around where the child sits.

- Share in the autistic child's interests and sense of humour and guide them gently through learning to focus on other things when they need to. Try not to chat when they are concentrating, learning to pause and be quiet when you need to is an important skill so that you do not overload or distract the attention of your autistic pupil.

- When autistic children seem very reliant on you, that is a good sign that they feel safe with you. **Don't try to wean them off a good relationship without replacing it with someone equally as safe and reliable**. If they struggle when you are not with them, write a reassuring story for them with instructions for the replacement person on how you work well together. If you know you might be off for an appointment or training course, prepare the child in advance, give clear instructions to the person covering you or a clear account of the day if no one will be with the child. This will be when the relationship with the class teacher is most important and should be just as strong and secure for the child so that they can manage that time without the 1:1 TA.

Mohammed has two teaching assistants that take turns to look after him for the whole time he is in school. He is autistic and has Pathological Demand Avoidance (PDA) and for a long time would struggle to access any of the regular curriculum. He spent a lot of time outside the classroom, worrying and becoming very distressed when demands to go back to class were put on him.

At the beginning of Year 5, the TAs met with the new class teacher and agreed to work as a team, with the class teacher looking for ways that Mohammed would be able to join in the class lesson, harnessing his interests, which happened to be maths.

The teacher started to give Mohammed the opportunity to be the maths expert who gave the right answer to the daily maths challenge. He loved this and it became the highlight of the day. On top of this, the class teacher began to make reference to Mohammed's interests during his class teaching time, giving him lots of fun and humour when he accepted the challenge to notice when this was happening. The teaching assistants could then harness this and respond to the lesson content checking what he knew and had learned in the 1:1 time that followed. This has made a huge impact on Mohammed's willingness to come to school and his ability to be at school.

14

SOCIAL SUPPORT

Almost every autistic child that I have worked with in primary schools has struggled with anxiety or their mental health because of the sensory, social and emotional challenges of being at school. The autistic brain, working on a different operating system, can struggle to understand the social cues that are going on all around them. Autistic people might struggle to put together all the parts of the bigger picture, i.e., context, which includes facial expressions, body language, meaning and inference in words, and understanding the situation around what just happened.

> The most significant trust-related challenge for people with autism is trusting other people. Most of us are neurologically hardwired with the ability to predict the behaviour of others – to read body language intuitively and make subconscious judgments based on how relaxed a person's body is, on how a person looks at other people, or by the social context. But that is often more difficult for people with autism. Ros Blackburn explains that she lives every day trying to understand people's intentions when they approach her. "Because I find it so difficult to predict the behavior of other people," Ros explains, "what they do often comes across as very sudden and threatening to me."
>
> *(Prizant, 2022)*

Bill Mason (2014) talks about how autistic young people can feel that everybody else has a kind of telepathy that they don't have because others seem to know what's happening

DOI: 10.4324/9781003280064-17

and what that means. The most illuminating research is being done by Dr Damian Milton and those using his Double Empathy Problem. This explains that, whilst autistic people may find reading other people's social cues difficult, the same could be said for neurotypical people reading autistic social cues. The problem is that we're always evaluating social interaction based on a neurotypical perspective. Autistic young people often have their own ways of interacting and socialising which, when allowed to do so, leads to strong and comfortable relationships with others. I run an after-school group for autistic young people and it has been a joy to see how they work their own ways of interacting with each other. Sometimes that is just being alongside each other, at other times it is sharing their experiences. Often it is just doing fun activities that they are enjoying doing together, such as making a very chocolatey Rocky Road cake!

In schools we enforce neurotypical socialisation as the norm and then label children who don't behave in the way we expect as having problems. The social challenges for autistic children are constant: from the morning playground full of parents and children, there is no break from social demands throughout the school day. Even times when other children may be relaxed and having down time, such as playtimes, there is no oasis for the autistic child. Even those autistic children who have good friendships and enjoy being with their friends might long for some space and time to be on their own to recharge their batteries when socialising becomes too much.

> I wish my friends would understand that when I want to be on my own it's not because I don't like them, it's because I am exhausted with trying to be just like them. But then I end up staying with them because I don't want them to make comments about me and it's all too much. My mum tends to get it all when I get home. I am often really horrible to her, but I don't mean it, it's just all that tension coming out.
>
> (Autistic child, aged ten)

Some children have been extremely fortunate in having a school experience that has supported them and enabled them to make strong friendships. Many more autistic children tell me they are overwhelmed, misunderstood and often bullied in primary school.

There are many social skills programmes that promise to teach autistic children the skills they need to fit into the neurotypical world. It is true that learning some 'social context reading' can be very successful for autistic children, but only if it is done to build their confidence and other people understand and learn their way of socialising too. It is equally useful for neurotypical children to learn about autistic and other neurodivergent ways of interacting. Otherwise, all we do is pile the pressure onto the autistic child to change who they are, to do all the work and teach them that they are the ones who have got it wrong.

Here are some ideas to support social confidence with autistic and other children.

- Teaching autistic students about autistic ways of communicating and researching autistic role models for them can be empowering and give them a sense of pride in who they are. This can counteract all the negative messages that they are given about who they are being 'wrong.'
- We need to be careful how we measure their social confidence and make sure that the child's own perspective and desires are included in how we measure any success. I use a lot of self-evaluation, asking the child where they feel more confident and the effect that has had on their wellbeing.
- It can be useful to think about what we are teaching and why. There are social rules that are cultural, such as giving eye contact or how to greet someone. These rules are different in different cultures – just think how many different cultural backgrounds there may be in a school population. But there are also social cooperation skills, and these enable us to work out how to get along with each other and work together.

- We can explore what skills a group will need to cooperate with each other on a shared interesting activity. We use structured and shared activities that the children enjoy (there's no value in doing something they're not enjoying), and these can be board games and card games, Lego, crafts, gardening, writing or projects that we share some interest in.
- We can develop this into exploring ways of managing social interactions with neurotypical and other neurodivergent people, and build up their ability to be able to advocate for themselves. This might be learning to say no or how to get out of a situation that makes them feel uncomfortable. It might be being able to explain to their friends what being autistic means to them.
- There are many resources that you can use but we find some clear visuals of the agreed focus, simple Social Stories that explain the skill in an autism-friendly way, and clear structure help us the most. When the children are invested in the group, they tend to come up with lots of amazing ideas that drive our planning. I have included some autism-friendly resources in the Resources section.

> *No matter how hard I try to learn from other people or copy what others are doing, I can't quite get it right. It's like living in a foreign country and not knowing the language.*
> *(Rosie King, livingautism.com)*

If we take autistic children out of class to do 'social skills' we are in danger of isolating them further from their peers. We need to think this through. Would you take a group of Black children out of class to learn white culture? Small groups of activity-based sessions where the adult works with a mix of children to help the children work out how to work together, understand each other and help each other can be much more successful. Learning to respect differences should be high on any school's approach and curriculum. Resources such as the Learning about Neurodiversity at School (LEANS) project are also in the Resources section.

It's hard to filter when there are lots of other sounds going on, e.g., 'background noise' as well as the conversation I'm meant to be a part of. I feel like I end up processing everything ... it's very stressful, irritating and overwhelming.
(Alis Rowe, livingautism.com)

PLAYTIMES

Playtimes can be a relief, or they can be the most difficult time of the day for autistic pupils. It's unstructured time, which some like as there are no demands, and others hate as they might not know what to do or how to fill the time. It's also a time and place where the sensory stimulation is different from in the classroom. Some autistic children love it because they are sensory seekers and need the movement and sensory stimulation. Others hate it because the sights, sounds, smells, noise, weather, movement, touch and space of a playground hurt their sensory sensitivities. Playtimes are socially demanding. Many autistic children don't like playtimes because there's a lot to take in; children are moving and talking and shouting and playing and coming at them from all directions. They might not know where to start to even ask to play, and possibly no one asks them to play.

Often in games being played, the rules keep changing, so when they thought they were playing one game someone changes it to another, just like that, and they can't keep up and are left behind, or get angry because someone changed the rules and that is stressful beyond words. There's no place to escape at playtimes and often no choice of whether you go outside or not. Some autistic children will wander, trying to find their own bit of space where they can just be on their own. Others will invent their own worlds to escape to so the noise and mess around them can be shut out. It's scary and it's easy to feel angry. Children are running, screaming and pushing. Imagine an autistic child who is frightened because they don't know how to join in without getting it wrong. Hitting out at others is just getting them out of the way, or attempting to join in when you can't communicate so well. Even though an autistic

DOI: 10.4324/9781003280064-18

child may look like they're doing OK and joining in, the effort is exhausting. You notice it when they come back into class, especially in the afternoon. Or maybe it's their parents who find out when they go home and it all comes out.

To help autistic children at playtimes:

- Take some time to go outside and watch what they do. See where they go and how they play. Do they approach other children? How do other children react to them?
- Be mindful of those children that mask. They will initially seem OK, and it is easy to assume that there are no difficulties for them. To find out more, we will need to listen in and ask the parents about what the child says at home. We may need to personally ask the child, giving them permission to be honest with us.
- For those who are keen to fit in and not be different, we may need to find subtle ways of giving them a break and make that socially plausible to help them feel that they are not being singled out.

PLAYTIMES AND OUTDOOR PLAY IN THE EARLY YEARS

- Some autistic children may want to be outside all the time, in all weathers and for them, that outdoor space feels like the safest part of the school. They are getting the sensory input they need and space away from the demands of the classroom.
- Transitions between the indoor and outdoor spaces might be difficult for them and we should make clear where they are going and why, and give them time to process the transition.
- If we understand the child's sensory needs, we can take what they like about both spaces into the other space. For example, if they like standing on a log outside or hiding under a shelter, then we can create similar spaces inside to provide that safe and familiar place to be.
- It may be that autistic children need some clear visual prompts to know what is accessible to them and when.

- Be consistent and consider whether the child should have more access to the space they feel most comfortable with. In one of my schools, autistic children were enabled to access whichever part of the indoor or outside space they needed to at the beginning of the year and they were gradually introduced to other areas as they felt calm and regulated, and had built up the trust with the class staff.

PRIMARY PLAYTIMES

When playtimes are timetabled and not accessible during the lessons, autistic children can often be left to their own devices. It's only when their behaviour becomes noticeable that teachers might notice a difficulty and end up reacting to that rather than seeing the challenges that the child has had all along. Assessing the experience of playtimes for the child will take some time. When I do this with autistic children I will go and observe them in the playground, including the transition from the classroom to the outdoor area and back to the classroom. Some children may be found rescuing insects from the edges of the grassy area; others may focus on joining in a football game and being in control of that; some may gather younger children together and organise a play activity with them in charge, and others may fawn and follow a group of peers in order not to be picked on or through fear of not knowing what to do. Some may wander the perimeters of the playground, humming to themselves or hiding away in a corner, or may stick closely to the adult on duty despite repeated encouragements to "go and find someone to play with."

- Give them some time to be alone, inside if necessary. Some children need this. Don't force them to be sociable and interact with others if it is causing them so much stress. They might like to just do nothing in particular, do a sensory calming activity or play with some of their favourite toys. They might like to do certain jobs, such as tidying the library or sorting out the Lego. They might find this helps them cope better with the rest of the day.

- Assess how anxious playtime is making the child. This will indicate what you may need to do. If anxiety is high, don't ignore it. Staying in or letting them have a break from inter-action may be the best thing you can do to help them regu-late their anxiety. For others, a TA to support them might be what they need and that makes them feel safer and happier. For others, supporting them and the other children to play together well might be what they need.
- Some children benefit from building in some structure. Work with the child to find ways of structuring the play-times. It could be a choice of five-minute activities. It could be a choice of one from a set of game bags that they can play with a friend (Jenny Mosley's playtime books have some great ideas about these).

When Caleb showed interest in playing football, he used to run onto the pitch and pick up the ball, then run away with it as the other children chased him. He wanted to join in but had not quite grasped the rules of the game. We enlisted a couple of older children to teach the rules and skills of football to Caleb over a half term, giving them 10-15 minutes a few times a week to do so in the hall or quiet playground. Parents started to watch football matches on TV with him and found 'how to play' videos on YouTube for him to watch. Slowly, over the year, Caleb became a footballer.

- Involve sensory movement activities, or any sensory activi-ties that the child may use and is part of their sensory diet, if they have one. Get other children to join in. For example, a sensory-seeking child may love to have a group of children doing a sensory circuit (see resources) with them on the playground equipment.
- Think carefully before using a TA to supervise 1:1 at play-times. Why are they there? What is their role? Is it to help

the child learn skills they want to learn, or to prompt them about behaviour? Is the TA going to be spending the time telling the child off, or modelling to other children how to interact well with the child?

- Have a buddy group. It depends on the child and their desire to have people they can play with. Ideally a buddy group is supported through sessions where they work out what they all like to play and discuss what to do if someone doesn't want to play and how to help each other to have an enjoyable playtime.
- Have breaktime clubs. Those that cover the particular interests of the autistic children work well. In primary schools, I have helped set up dinosaur, Mario and Lego clubs, games clubs and computer clubs.
- Make a plan for wet playtimes – have a quiet space, a favoured activity and some choice of whether to be in the class or another calmer space.

> *It's not that we're born with social anxiety; we develop it as a form of self-protection. I think our social anxiety stems from our difficulty in understanding social situations and from years of social blunders and missteps that often result in us being misunderstood, judged, mistreated, ridiculed, and bullied.*
>
> *(Siena Castellon, 2020, p. 91)*

BULLYING

It's not that I don't want to make friends, but that the other children don't want to be my friend.

(Autistic child, aged nine)

Well for my whole primary school life I was bullied and tormented to the point when I tried cutting myself. Schools always said they would deal with things and the only way things would be dealt with is with them isolating me away from the bullies. I don't see why I should be isolated for reporting bullying???

(Autistic child, Spectrum Gaming)

A recent study reported 62% of autistic children had experienced bullying such as being deliberately provoked into meltdown, sensory bullying, social exclusion, their social naivety being taken advantage of, and cyber-bullying, including fake accounts, public shaming and Photoshopping (IAN 2014). Sadly, my team of autism specialist teachers and I listen to stories of these happening to many of our autistic pupils. And the worrying thing is that it often starts in primary school. In my work with the anti-bullying charity, Kidscape, we have heard so many stories of autistic children being bullied because they are different and seen as an easy target. Autistic children and their parents often report that schools did not believe them, even blaming the autistic child for bringing it upon themselves. Picking out the autistic child in class and making them an object of ridicule in front of the other children is also a form of bullying by adults that we need to beware of. I wish I did not have to write that. I wish I did not have to listen to the ways that autistic children are picked on, left out, persecuted and hurt because they are

DOI: 10.4324/9781003280064-19

different. It is often the autistic children who are called 'weird,' imitated when they stim and even tormented by children who know that a certain noise or action is hated by the autistic child. It is far rarer for an autistic child to be the bully, and, as seen earlier with the story about the girl who hit her TA, there are often anxieties and trauma at the root of their behaviour which we can work through.

> When girls are annoying they are just a little bit mean, a little bit snide and it goes on and on. Then they act nice afterwards and get away with it.
>
> *(Autistic child, aged 11)*

Autistic children seem to be more at risk of being bullied when they attempt to join in and make friends. Their lack of confidence in navigating the social world at school can be picked up on by other children who laugh and make fun of them. They can then become easy targets.

> First, we need to understand that autistic children are generally very honest, and very accurate. Few invent stories to get another child into difficulty, and few invent things that have not happened. So, our first step is to presume competence and say that we will take what they say seriously and investigate it properly.
>
> *(Ann Memmott, autistic adult, 2018)*

To help a child and their parents when they report bullying:

- Use a visual communication system. There are resources and advice on www.kidscape.org.uk/advice/advice-for-parents-and-carers/what-is-bullying/autistic-children-and-bullying/, which has symbol-based communication mats and strategies to help based on schools and parents working together to make the bullying stop.
- Ask parents to keep a diary of the child's reports of what is happening. Ask them to report facts and how their child interpreted the situation. Reassure them you believe

them and set a time to meet for after you have done more investigation.

- Talk to the other children involved but instead of accusing them, ask them about what sort of games they play, how they deal with conflict and what problems they have with each other. Often the bullying is other children picking up on the differences and making fun of the autistic child, but also the reactions of the autistic child are sometimes misinterpreted by the other children and vice versa. This is where the LEANS resources could help.

- There can be misunderstandings and misinterpretation by the autistic child and the other children involved. Sometimes drawing the story out in a comic strip, using speech and thought bubbles, can help show what happened and what was misinterpreted.

- Bring all the information together and try to share the whole picture with parents without blame. Where reactions and words are malicious, deal with them and teach children what is acceptable and what is not. This does not have to be teaching them that their classmate is autistic, but can be generally about neurodiversity and difference. Where misinterpretation has happened, deal with that through visual comic strips or clear explanations for the autistic child and the other children.

- Try to repair relationships. If the autistic child cannot cope with the other children because of the hurt and anxiety they have caused, then give them time and support them in making new relationships through common interests, shared activities and successful projects. For example, one child built confidence and new friendships by joining the eco-committee at school.

EMOTIONS AND ANXIETY SUPPORT

We can use many different ways of trying to get children to communicate how they are feeling, such as weather-based emotion boards where children put a peg onto the cloud or sunshine to say how they are feeling. So many autistic children have told me they hate these, or just put their peg on the sunshine (or their favourite colour), that the whole thing is meaningless at best and stress-inducing at worst. These methods can cause problems because autistic children may be anxious for others not to know how they are feeling or constantly confused about how they are feeling (alexithymia). Are you ever only feeling one emotion? How quickly do emotions come and go? Can you feel bad and good at the same time? Of course we can! (And yes, somewhere will be an autistic child who loves the weather feelings chart; all autistic children are different!) Many autistic people say they are very aware of other people's feelings and have a lot of empathy, but can struggle to process or communicate a response. Other autistic people can have hyper-sensitivity to their interoception system and every emotion is a huge physical event in their bodies. These differences will show themselves in different responses and reactions in the person's behaviour. In some people this may be seen in external behaviours, such as big reactions and distress due to seemingly small emotional events. Others could internalise those reactions, becoming more anxious and withdrawn. Anxiety is the most commonly reported emotion in the children we support. But sometimes alexithymia means that they are interpreting all emotions as anxiety as they have not yet learned to recognise the differences between different emotions.

DOI: 10.4324/9781003280064-20

> *I am either really happy or really angry, sad or worried. I can tell them apart but only when they are really strong. This means I don't always know what I feel and what I'm upset about.*
>
> *(Rose Smitten, 2021)*

> *I avoid telling people that I frequently don't know how I'm feeling. I don't know how to describe how I'm feeling. I suspect that most people would find this baffling ... My emotions rarely matched my facial expressions and body language, this often leads to misunderstandings ... I find it frustrating because the facial expressions or those attributed to me rarely reflect my mood. I am constantly being misunderstood.*
>
> *(Siena Castellon, 2020, pp. 88, 89.)*

What we can do to support autistic pupils with their emotions:

- Make sure first and foremost that it isn't something that you or others are doing that is causing the anxiety. This includes poor support, poor communication and not recognising their autism needs. It includes looking out for bullying and social isolation. Anxiety is not always the child's issue but can be the result of others' poor understanding and support.
- Check out their sensory sensitivities. This is the first port of call for me as sensory issues can be the source of most of an autistic person's emotional reactions. Remember it can take time for an autistic child, young person or adult to recognise their own sensory differences and process the sensory information coming into their brains.
- We mustn't expect the child to be in control of their emotions, but do teach them how emotions affect us and explore what they are like inside, the physical responses as well as the thoughts and feelings. "The Incredible 5-Point Scale" is a good visual resource for some autistic children and young people. There is something else that they should be taught too: that we can seek out trusted others to help us regulate (feel better).

- Acknowledge their feelings. They are real. I have a saying: "emotions are real, even if they are not always telling us the truth." Dismissing them only teaches a child that they need to hide or suppress their feelings and that can lead to mental ill health, even in primary school children.

- Teach problem-solving, and use a visual map to show you are listening and how all the elements of what they are feeling link to facts. Remember that, for autistic children, their perspectives can feel like fact to them. They can struggle to adapt their thoughts and be very frightened of unknown or unpredictable situations.

- Work regularly on understanding what 'calm' feels like for them. Calm is a better baseline than 'happy.' Finding ways that help us manage anxiety and change it into 'calm' or just 'OK' is OK. Coming alongside the child and trying things out, maybe recording what experiences help them feel better, does take time.

- You can help by making talking about emotions part of your everyday life and having a commentary on your emotions.

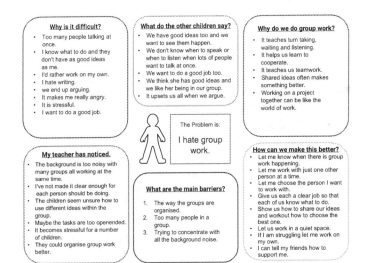

Why is it difficult?
- Too many people talking at once.
- I know what to do and they don't have as good ideas as me.
- I'd rather work on my own.
- I hate writing.
- we end up arguing.
- It makes me really angry.
- It is stressful.
- I want to do a good job.

What do the other children say?
- We have good ideas too and we want to see them happen.
- We don't know when to speak or when to listen when lots of people want to talk at once.
- We want to do a good job too.
- We think she has good ideas and we like her being in our group.
- It upsets us all when we argue.

Why do we do group work?
- It teaches turn taking, waiting and listening.
- It helps us learn to cooperate.
- It teaches us teamwork.
- Shared ideas often makes something better.
- Working on a project together can be like the world of work.

My teacher has noticed.
- The background is too noisy with many groups all working at the same time.
- I've not made it clear enough for each person should be doing.
- The children seem unsure how to use different ideas within the group.
- Maybe the tasks are too openended.
- It becomes stressful for a number of children.
- They could organise group work better.

The Problem is:
I hate group work.

What are the main barriers?
1. The way the groups are organised.
2. Too many people in a group.
3. Trying to concentrate with all the background noise.

How can we make this better?
- Let me know when there is group work happening.
- Let me work with just one other person at a time.
- Let me choose the person I want to work with.
- Give us each a clear job so that each of us know what to do.
- Show us how to share our ideas and workout how to choose the best one.
- Let us work in a quiet space.
- If I am struggling let me work on my own.
- I can tell my friends how to support me.

Figure 17.1 Problem-solving example.

Simply say things like, "I'm tired and it's making me a bit grumpy. I'm going to have a rest to make me feel better."

MELTDOWNS AND SHUTDOWNS

"An overwhelming response to an intense situation."
(www.autism.org.uk)

A meltdown or a shutdown is the brain's reaction to extreme sensory, communication and social overload. It's not a perfect picture but one autistic person described it as a computer crash. If you've ever had a computer crash on you, you know that the processor freezes. No matter how many buttons you press, it can't do anything. It cannot take any more input. You have to switch it off and let it reboot.

Meltdowns, where the child is trying to run away, lying on the floor, maybe hitting out, throwing things or screaming, are a reaction to a brain crash. The child is in extreme distress and the brain has entered into 'fight or flight' mode. The ultimate purpose is to keep the person safe by fighting or fleeing. But that is not a conscious decision, it is instinct.

But there is also the 'freeze' response. This is where the brain shuts down and the person cannot move or withdraws into a safer place. Often autistic people say that they cannot control, function or even remember what happens when they are in meltdown or shutdown. It is meltdowns we see because they are usually visible. Those who have shutdowns are often missed. But shutdowns may be much more common. Less commonly known is the 'fawn' response. This is when the person becomes an extreme people pleaser in order to minimise the fear and panic they are suffering. We can easily interpret this as a 'model pupil' and miss the extreme anxiety the child is masking.

> *It seems that a huge number of autistic people have shutdowns …*
>
> *What's a shutdown like? I can explain mine. If you put me under intense social and sensory stress, my brain starts*

to feel disorientated. I lose the ability to talk. I can some-times write, though that ability gets very erratic the worse it becomes. I lose the ability to work out how to look after myself, or get myself home in busy streets. There is a sen-sation of great internal brain-pain/fuzziness. Things can look weirdly big/small when it's happening. Afterwards, I'm totally exhausted and need to recover for a good hour and a half, often longer. It's not in my control, at all.

(Ann Memmott, autistic adult)

To help a child who may have meltdowns or shutdowns, at school or at home after school, we need to connect the dots between their school stress and the transition to being at home. Blaming teachers or parents or worse, the child, is common, but unnecessary. If we work together to provide the understanding and support the child needs, by going through the strategies in this book for example, then we are more likely to prevent many meltdowns or shutdowns. When I work in schools, we start from understanding the extreme distressed state of the child and working out how to reduce that stress. Then we usually see a reduction in meltdowns. It works.

But here is how I would support a child who is having a melt-down or shutdown:

- **Remove all possible sensory stressors**. These can be peo-ple or objects; it could involve turning the lights down, or seeing if the child will go to a quiet and safe place (prefer-ably you have shown and prepared a place beforehand that they will know is safe for them when they are in distress).
- **Keep talk to a minimum**. Talking is sensory overload and often makes the child even more angry and distressed. If in doubt – just be silent.
- **Be patient and give them time to recover**. Reassure them they are not in trouble, that you will help them get through this. Say something like, "I am here for you, we can talk later." Tell them that things can be repaired. But don't talk too much. Some autistic children need the rest of the day to recover; some may feel OK after a shorter time.

- **Repair only once they have recovered**. Reassure them that they are not to blame and that you understand something went wrong that was out of their control. Discuss gently what you can do to help them feel better or repair a relationship with another person they may have hurt (this should include the other person acknowledging how the autistic person felt too). As adults, some humility and acknowledgement that we may have contributed can go a long way.
- **Support and plan ahead**. Work as a team with your class staff, Special Educational Needs Co-ordinator (SENCO) and parents to put a support plan in place as you learn how to prevent and avoid meltdowns for the child.

Frequent meltdowns in schools are often interpreted as tantrums or bad behaviour. With sanctions and punishments piling up, exclusions and anxiety growing on the part of everyone, it can lead to permanent exclusions and autistic children who end up out of school, severely traumatised by the whole school experience. There are a growing number of autistic children who are not able to manage school at all, following placements where they were not understood and their behaviour was labelled as naughty and deliberate. Looking at behaviour through an autism lens illuminates our perceptions of their visible behaviours and enables us to see the communication, sensory, social, emotional and learning difficulties they may be struggling with. We can work to make these things better for them.

And one last thought … if the child has not yet received a diagnosis and you think they may be autistic – assess those needs and make those accommodations. You won't harm them and you can monitor what works and what doesn't as part of the Graduated Approach towards a fuller understanding of their needs. The strategies in this book can help children with other needs, those with attachment needs, trauma, anxiety and other neurodiverse conditions.

TRANSITIONS

There are different kinds of transitions and thinking about each will help you support your autistic child through these. Transitions, that is, moving to a new situation, can be difficult for autistic children for different reasons. Sometimes it is because they have missed a cue, or didn't realise that the instruction was for them. They may be fully involved in one activity and struggle to come out of it to move their attention to another activity. You may not have explained it in a way they understand, and they may need more information than most children so that they can manage the new thing. Some autistic children have a wave of anxiety so strong that it can paralyse them, and they may refuse, shutdown or meltdown with the overwhelming challenge. What seems like a manageable activity for most children in your class may need much more support for an autistic child.

DAILY TRANSITIONS

We may not realise that the day to day moving from one activity to the next can pose a challenge for many autistic children. In the early years, I notice that autistic children can be lost in the continuous provision, not knowing how to move from activity to activity, and then when the teacher says, "now we will all do this" (such as come to the carpet), they cannot manage it. Cues we use to lead children through our daily routines may be missed by autistic children. Another difficulty some report is that we don't do things when we say we will and that uncertainty can again cause anxiety. This difficulty with transitions can continue right through the primary years, even before they face the transition to high school.

DOI: 10.4324/9781003280064-21

- Giving an autistic child a clear lead up, communicating what they are moving to, and allowing them time to process the change will be much more effective. I once worked with a child who needed a good five minutes of warning before any transition. We needed to say what the next thing was and then leave him to process the instruction. After five minutes, he would get up and do the next thing.
- Make the transition positive, smooth and calm. So many transitions I observe in primary schools are chaotic, noisy and busy. An autistic child could be given a very specific task to do, for example tidying up the same small and specific thing every day, or doing a specific job for the teacher at that time.

TRANSITION TO A NEW CLASS

Every year we work with our pupils to prepare them for the next school year, and this often means a new teacher and a new classroom. One thing we always advise is to think about **what will be familiar to the child** first. If we understand that generally people cope with change by drawing on familiar past experiences, then it may be that we need to help an autistic child connect to these, as it is difficult for them to do so.

- Positive regular visits to the new class to get to know the teacher in the term before the change can be really helpful. Remember that your classroom will not look exactly the same, and the autistic child will notice, so think about what you can do just before they return after the summer holidays.
- A booklet about moving to the next class can be made which has pictures and information for the child to take home in the school holidays and make the change seem more familiar (see Resources chapter).
- Teachers can send photos or a video of their classroom, or put them on the school website, just before the new term begins, so it will be exactly how it will be on the first day of term.
- Email the first day's timetable to the family on your inset day and make sure the child has familiar items in the place

they will be sitting. Remind them of the place they will keep their things and the support you will be giving them. And if you can, relate it to their particular enthusiasms so they know you are mindful of the things that are important to them.

- You could arrange an earlier start so the autistic child can orientate themselves in the new class before the other children come in. Some schools allow the Special Educational Needs and Disabilities (SEND) children to come in with their parents on the days before school starts, again to help them make that transition.

- Be mindful that settling in may take longer for autistic children. Feeling safe is the most important thing for them. Explain everything well enough and often enough until they do feel OK with it and make whatever sensory and organisational adjustments that will enable them to be able to do things. Even when you have maybe 30 other children to teach in your class, this approach helps more children than you may realise.

TRANSITION AT THE END OF PRIMARY SCHOOL

Going to high school is a huge change and often a huge worry for parents of autistic children. The daily transitions of moving from teacher to teacher around a much bigger school, the transitions to travelling to school and homework are a challenge for many. However, a good secondary school will take charge of the transition and work with the family and primary school to do as much as they can to make the transition work. If the child doesn't have an Individual Education Plan (IEP) or Education, Health and Care Plan (EHCP) then you will need to pass on the information about the child's needs and adaptations that help them in a clear format. Any reports from outside professionals done in the past two years can help, especially if they mentioned the considerations needed for transition.

Making it as familiar as possible for the autistic child is going to help. Extra visits, video and photos of key people and places, a map, a sample timetable and help with understanding the different rules and routines. If there are extra taster days or even a summer school, then take the opportunity to help the child get used to the environment and how a high school works. I have worked with many secondary schools and helped with the transition of many autistic children and have put a booklet together that you can download to collect all the relevant information (see Resources chapter). Many autistic children do make a good transition if the support is there within the high school. The key for parents is to get to know the Learning Support department head (this may or may not be the SENCO) and find out what happens in reality on a daily basis.

Primary teachers can do some helpful things that can support this transition. Here are our top tips:

- Start using a whole week visual timetable so that the child can get used to working out where they are in the week (the whole class will benefit from doing this). This scanning of the timetable and being able to get the equipment they need for the lesson is great practice for high school.
- We often make a year-long timeline at the beginning of the year. On it, we will add the key events, holidays, trips, birthdays, SATS and the end of the year, marked in months. At the beginning of the final year at primary school, so many people start talking about tests and transitions that it can seem imminent to an autistic child. Seeing the timeline can ease some of that pressure.
- If an autistic child has had a 1:1 TA with them, then the provision may still be there in their EHCP, but high schools tend to use TAs differently. The child is likely to have to work with different TAs in different subjects. Start to extend the people the child might work with but clearly communicate who they will work with and when, and if possible, enable them to start and end the day with someone familiar. The same can be done by going to different classrooms for some lessons if this is possible in the size of your primary school.
- Remember to live in the moment too. The last year of primary school can be very special and a time to celebrate all your child has achieved. I know for some it won't have been

a good experience and they can't wait to start afresh at high school, or even never want to go to school again; however, many will feel sad and want to stay with the familiar people who have looked after them all those years.

- Keep a routine and keep anchoring their day in familiar things, even after SATS. Use that visual timetable, prepare them for new experiences and trips well, and they can have a successful last year at primary school.

> *My daughter was so fed up of all the 'exciting and new' things the class were going to do after the SATS that she stood up in the middle of assembly and shouted "I want my lessons back!" She needed the regular and familiar and fortunately the teachers saw this and put maths and English back on the timetable, and let all the children do these subjects related to something they were interested in.*
>
> *(Parent of autistic child)*

FURTHER ADVICE AND RESOURCES

I understand that, as teachers, we need understanding, but we also need resources. When someone has created a good resource that we can use for our pupils, it can save us time and help them learn in the way that works best for them. There are thousands of resources out there and some of them will be just right for your autistic pupil, and many will not be. I hope that after reading this book you will be able to better pick out what will be an affirming and positive resource for your autistic child, and what to leave well alone!

I have a website, am on Twitter and have a Facebook page where I post trusted resources that I find from my networks and internet searches, and some that we make ourselves. If you'd like to join me, here are the links:

https://reachoutasc.com
https://twitter.com/ReachoutASC
www.facebook.com/ReachoutASC

SOME GOOD AUTISM WEBSITES

https://autisticnotweird.com
www.differentjoy.com
www.pdasociety.org.uk
www.scottishautism.org

SOME GOOD AUTISM RESOURCES, BOOK LISTS, VISUALS, TEACHING PACKS

https://autisticgirlsnetwork.org/resources/
https://chatterpack.net
www.ed.ac.uk/salvesen-research/leans
www.autismeducationtrust.org.uk/resources

DOI: 10.4324/9781003280064-22

https://best-practice.middletownautism.com
www.griffinot.com/asd-and-sensory-processing-disorder/
https://reachoutasc.com/resources/
https://occupationaltherapy.com.au/the-top-10-books-on
    -sensory-processing/
https://padlet.com/spectrumgaming/AutismResources

COMMUNICATION RESOURCES

www.talkingmats.com/talking-mats-in-action/for-education/
www.routledge.com/Colourful-Semantics-A-Resource-for
    -Developing-Childrens-Spoken-and-Written/Forth-Valley
    /p/book/9780367210502?utm_source=cjaffiliates&utm
    _medium=affiliates&cjevent=5b32bab5556111ed83d0736
    b0a18ba74
https://shapecoding.com
http://thinkingtalking.co.uk/language-for-thinking/

SENSORY CHECKLIST AND SENSORY ACTIVITIES

www.sensorysmarts.com/sensory-checklist.pdf
www.boltonstartwell.org.uk/downloads/file/440/sensory
    -circuits

SOCIAL CONFIDENCE RESOURCES

https://ausometraining.com/product/autism-social-skills
    -konnect-bundle/
www.ed.ac.uk/salvesen-research/leans

OTHER LINKS

www.kidscape.org.uk/advice/advice-for-parents-and-carers/
    what-is-bullying/autistic-children-and-bullying/
www.autisticslt.com/nd-affirmingslt
https://monotropism.org/in-practice/#school
www.spectrumgaming.net
www.nurseryworld.co.uk/features/article/eyfs-best-practice
    -all-about-autism

PLAYTIME IDEAS BY JENNY MOSLEY

www.circle-time.co.uk/product-category/pocket-books/

TRANSITION BOOKLETS

https://reachoutasc.com/wp-content/uploads/2021/05/
Transition-to-new-class-2021.pdf

https://reachoutasc.com/wp-content/uploads/2020/08/Rea
choutASCtransitiontoSecondaryschoolbooklet.pdf

BIBLIOGRAPHY

Autistic Not Weird (2017) https://autisticnotweird.com/sats/

Beardon, L (2019) *Autism and Asperger Syndrome in Childhood For Parents and Carers of the Newly Diagnosed – Overcoming Common Problems*. Pub: John Murray Press.

Blackburn, R (2021) https://slideplayer.com/slide/4221171/

Bobb, V (2019) Girls and Autism. In Carpenter, B, Happe, F, & Egerton, J (Eds), *Educational, Family and Personal Perspectives*. Pub: Routledge, 36–47.

Bryan, J (2018) *Eye Can Write: A Memoir of a Child's Silent Soul Emerging*. Pub: Bonnier Books Ltd.

Castellon, S (2020) *The Spectrum Girl's Survival Guide: How to Grow Up Awesome and Autistic*. Pub: JKP.

Conn, C (2015) 'Sensory highs', 'vivid rememberings' and 'interactive stimming': Children's play cultures and experiences of friendship in autistic autobiographies, *Disability & Society*, 30:8, 1192–1206, DOI: 10.1080/09687599.2015.1081094

Cullen, RL (2018) The autistic language hypothesis. https://www.researchgate.net/publication/327831058_Do_people_on_the_Autism_spectrum_have_an_over_reliance_on_verbal_communication_as_opposed_to_nonverbal_communication_body_language_and_facial_expressions_in_conversation

Denworth, L (2018) Spectrum News. https://www.spectrumnews.org/news/social-communication-autism-explained/

Diagnostic and Statistical Manual of Mental Disorders, Fifth Edition (DSM-5) criteria for diagnosing Autism. https://www.cdc.gov/ncbddd/autism/hcp-dsm.html

Education Endowment Foundation (2018) Making the best use of teaching assistants. https://educationendowmentfoundation.org.uk/education-evidence/guidance-reports/teaching-assistants

Forbes, H (2022) *How Autism May Affect Students' Understanding of Maths And What Teachers Can Do to Help.* https://thirdspacelearning.com/blog/autism-maths/

Gradin, T (2006). http://www.grandin.com/inc/visual.thinking.html

Gray, C (1994) *Comic Strip Conversations: Illustrated Interactions that Teach Conversation Skills to Students with Autism and Related Disorders.* Pub: Future Horizons.

Hanley, AJ, Khairat, M, Taylor, K, Wilson, R, Cole-Fletcher, R & Riby, D (2017) Classroom displays – attraction or distraction? Evidence of impact on attention and learning from children with and without autism. *Developmental Psychology,* 53. DOI: 10.1037/dev0000271

Higashida, N (2014) *The Reason I Jump: One Boy's Voice from the Silence of Autism.* Pub: Hodder & Stoughton.

https://livingautism.com/24-quotes-autistic-individuals/

https://www.autism.org.uk/what-we-do/help-and-support/how-to-talk-about-autism

https://www.cdc.gov/ncbddd/autism/hcp-dsm.html

https://www.nurseryworld.co.uk/features/article/eyfs-best-practice-all-about-autism

https://www.tandfonline.com/doi/pdf/10.1080/09687599.2017.1328157

International Autism Network (2014) https://iancommunity.org/cs/ian_research_reports/ian_research_report_bullying

Lees, E (nd) Why is 'Language Disorder' and 'Social Communication Disorder' problematic? https://www.autisticslt.com/faqs

Mason, W (2014) *The Autism Discussion Page an Anxiety, Behaviour, School, and Parenting Strategies.* Pub: JKP.

McCann, L (2019a) Social detectives pack. https://reachoutasc.com/resources/social-skills-pack/

McCann, L (2019b) *Stories that Explain.* Pub: LDA.

McCann, L and Kidscape (2022) https://www.kidscape.org.uk/advice/advice-for-parents-and-carers/what-is-bullying/autistic-children-and-bullying/

Mehrabian, A (1967) cited in: https://www.bl.uk/people/albert-mehrabian

Memmott, A (2016) http://annsautism.blogspot.com/2016/03/shutdown-autisms-hidden-majority.html

Memmott, A (2018) http://annsautism.blogspot.com/2018/12/

Mesibov, G (2015) *Accessing the Curriculum for Learners with Autism Spectrum Disorders: Using the TEACCH Programme to Help Inclusion.* Pub: Routledge.

Milton, D (2018) https://www.autism.org.uk/advice-and-guidance/professional-practice/double-empathy

Moss, H (2018) https://livingautism.com/24-quotes-autistic-individuals/

Mummytosix blog (2018) https://www.theplightofthesendparent.co.uk/teaching-assistants-and-children-with-special-educational-needs

Murray, D, Lesser, M, & Lawson, W (2005) Attention, monotropism and the diagnostic criteria for autism. *Autism: The International Journal of Research and Practice,* 9, 139–56. DOI: 10.1177/1362361305051398

National Autistic Society (nd) https://www.autism.org.uk/advice-and-guidance/what-is-autism/varying-support-needs

National Autistic Society (2006) On autism toolbox. http://www.autismtoolbox.co.uk/sites/default/files/resources/B_is_for_bullied%20National%20Autistic%20society.pdf

NICE Guidelines (2017) Autism spectrum disorder in under 19s: Recognition, referral and diagnosis. https://www.nice.org.uk/guidance/cg128

Prizant, B M with Tom Fields-Meyer (Revised and expanded edition) (2022) *Uniquely human – a different way of seeing Autism.* Pub: Simon & Schuster.

Robinson, S, Goddard, L, Dritschel, B, Wisley, M, & Howlin, P (2009) Executive functions in children with autism spectrum disorders. https://d1wqtxts1xzle7.cloudfront.net/46895006/Executive_functions_in_children_with_Aut20160629-8399

Sainsbury, C (2009) *Martian in the Playground: Understanding the Schoolchild With Asperger's Syndrome.* Pub: Lucky Duck Books.

Schuelka, MJ (2018) Implementing Inclusive Education. https://assets.publishing.service.gov.uk/media/5c6eb77340f0b647b214c599/374_Implementing_Inclusive_Education.pdf

SEND Code of Practice. (2014) https://www.gov.uk/government/publications/send-code-of-practice-0-to-25

Smitten, R (2021) *The Secret Life of Rose: Inside an Autistic Head.* Pub: Amazon.

Verhulst, I, MacLennan, K, Haffey, A, & Tavassoli, T (2022) The perceived casual relations between sensory reactivity differences and anxiety symptoms in autistic adults. *Autism in Adulthood,* 4:3, September 2022. https://www.liebertpub.com/doi/10.1089/aut.2022.0018

Vermueluen, P. (2012) Autism as context blindness. Pub: AAPC Publishing.

Watson, A (2022) https://www.learningandthebrain.com/blog/do-classroom-decorations-distract-students-a-story-in-4-parts-2/

Whelton, E (2021) https://ausometraining.com/aba-alternatives-social-skills/

Williams, D (1996) *Autism: An Inside-Out Approach: An Innovative Look at the 'Mechanics' of 'Autism' and its Developmental 'Cousins'.* Pub: JKP.

Woods, R (2017) Exploring how the social model of disability can be re-invigorated for autism. *Disability & Society*, 32(7), 1090–1095, DOI: 10.1080/09687599.2017.1328157

INDEX

Printed in the United States
by Baker & Taylor Publisher Services